CUT THE DECK

A step-by-step procedure for teaching writing

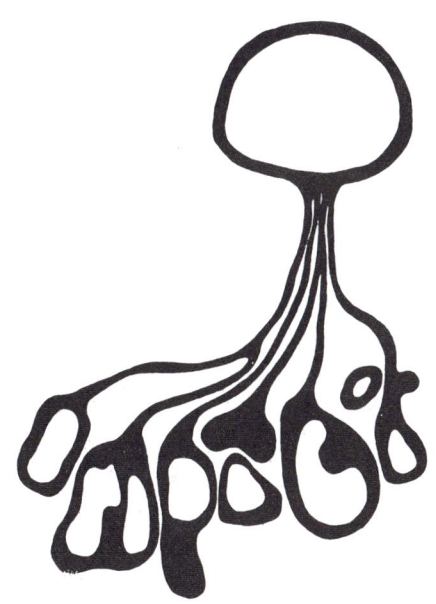

Robert B. Cahill and Herbert J. Hrebic

edited by
Jimi Barry

To all the students who have participated in the

Stack the Deck writing program,

this book is gratefully dedicated.

ACKNOWLEDGEMENTS

We would like to thank the following students who have contributed samples of their writing or served as readers in testing the materials: **David Anderson, Linas Bartuska, Mark Bleicher, Paul Cahill, Michael Carroll, Gerry Cebrzynski, Steve Dressel, Joseph Gavin, Stacia Hachem, Peter Kelly, Jerome Kohn, James Kupres, Gintaras Lietuvninkas, John Mulligan, Debbie Marciano, Patrick Mulligan, Kevin Marshall, Alex Ociepka, Thaddeus Okrzeskik, Michael Roman, Sarunas Rumsa, Chris Smith, James Florek, and Daniel Flens.**

We would also like to thank our associates and friends who helped in the development of the materials: **James Keleher, Bill Hogan, Marty Mongan, Linda Augustyn, Lorraine Pieja, Jack Carlson, Donald Augustyn, Bob Reidy, Bob Lyon, Diane Franchini, Sue Lagsdin,** and **Father Robert Sheridan.**

A special thanks to **Jimi Barry**, who edited the revised edition of **Cut the Deck.**

ISBN 0-933282-15-X

Copyright © 1985, 1979, 1977   REVISED EDITION

All rights reserved. This book, or parts thereof, may not be reproduced in any form without permission in writing from the publisher. Write **Stack the Deck, Inc.**, 9126 Sandpiper Ct., Orland Park, Illinois 60462.

INTRODUCTION

By the time you were four or five years old, you were able to carry on a conversation with many people about many subjects. While doing this you were naturally and automatically putting together the basic sounds of English into words, assigning meanings to these words, and combining these words into meaningful strings (sentences) in order to express your thoughts. As you concentrated on the thoughts themselves, you were unaware of how easily you used language. You learned all of this in a very short period of time without any formal schooling. You have such natural control of language that your capacity for producing sentences is infinite.

In accomplishing this feat, you were always putting parts of language together, never taking them apart. Frequently in putting these parts together, you did it in a way that no other speaker of the English language had done before. Without knowing it you have been using language in a very creative way.

This book is a writing composition book. Its main concern is to teach you how to write clearly and logically. Writing, unlike speech, is a learned art, not a natural one. Nature itself has shaped us to learn speech. Writing is a man-made invention which must be learned step-by-step. The central problem in learning how to write well is to discover as much as possible about the natural process by which we learn speech and then to convert this knowledge to learning how to write. This is exactly what **Cut the Deck** does.

The first unit is a confidence builder. You will explore and discover the amazing flexibility you have in using your language. You will find out that you are indeed a "walking grammar." The only materials you will need are **Cut the Deck** and yourself.

After the confidence building exercises, you will be raring to go onto the next ten units which deal with written composition.

The introductory units follow the natural process of oral language learning. They start with basic units of writing and teach the skills of putting these units together. You will learn how to combine these units, how to rearrange them, how to subtract those which are unnecessary, and finally how to expand them.

In learning these manipulatory skills, you will also discover the variety of options available to you for expressing the same idea. After mastering these skills, you will learn to apply them. Again you will discover the options open to you for organizing your thoughts. You will begin with simple organizational patterns and move onto complex ones. Gradually you will become a good writer, one who can automatically manipulate sentences into organizational patterns which best express the ideas you wish to communicate.

"No way," you say. Let's get started and see!

TABLE OF CONTENTS

Precomposing

1. Language Awareness 1
   Learning about the Language

2. Sentence Manipulation 11
   Four Sentence Writing Skills

3. Controlling Idea 33
   Learning the List Making Skill

Composing

Each organizational pattern follows a step-by-step procedure, including prewriting, writing, and rewriting activities.

4. How To Do Paper 41
   An Expository Composition Using the Command Form of the Verb

5. Personal Narrative Paper 55
   A Narrative Composition Using First Person Pronouns

6. Spatial Development Paper 75
   A Descriptive Composition

7. Personal Observation Paper 93
   A Narrative Composition Using Third Person Pronouns

8. Listing Paper 107
   An Expository Composition

9. An Order of Importance Paper 118
   An Argumentative Composition

10. Comparison-Contrast Paper 134
    An Expository-Argumentative Composition

11. Mood Paper 149
    An Expository-Descriptive Composition

UNIT ONE LANGUAGE AWARENESS

STUDENT LEARNING OBJECTIVES

1. The student will generate many sentences from a limited number of words.
2. The student will unscramble sentences.
3. The student will paraphrase never heard before sentences.
4. The student will understand multiple meanings in words.
5. The student will understand the multiple functions of words.
6. The student will coin new words.
7. The student will understand idioms.

You are a walking grammar! Without knowing it, you have mastered the rules of language as a young child without a teacher's instruction. If you didn't know these rules, you would not be able to speak.

The purpose of this first unit is to make you aware of how language works. We want to make you aware of what you know but might not know that you know! If that sounds confusing, it's really not. We simply want to show you how you use language automatically when you speak.

Your mind uses language in a remarkable way. As a young child with a small vocabulary, you spoke in thousands of sentences. You did this because of the spontaneous use your mind makes of language. The following exercises are designed to make you aware of this.

Language Machine

EXERCISE 1: As a group activity, see how many different sentences you can make up for the limited number of words given. Start at point "A" and follow the arrows. Use only the words listed.

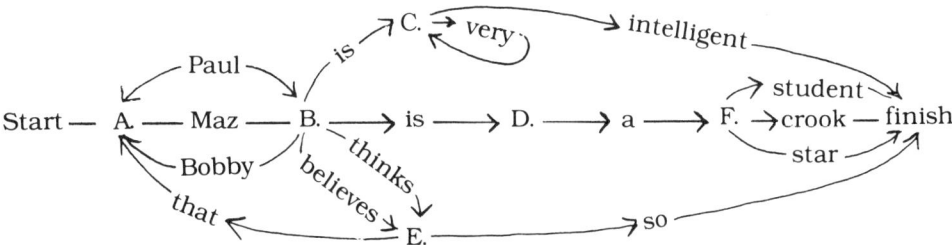

EXAMPLES:

1. Paul is a student.
2. Maz thinks that Paul is a crook.
3. Bobby is very intelligent.

Sentence Sense

You communicate to a listener all day long. A listener understands what you say because you put words in the right place. You have sentence sense.

Look at the following:

to   gave   biscuit   Ginger   a   her   hamster

That doesn't make sense, does it? Why? The words are out of order. Instead, you might say:

Ginger gave a biscuit to her hamster.

This makes sense. When you speak, you automatically put words in the right place. You function with the language. You might not know that a word is a noun, verb, past participle, or subordinating conjunction, but you use these words correctly in your everyday language.

EXERCISE 2: On a separate sheet of paper, unscramble the scrambled words. Arrange them in an order that makes sentence sense. Your sentences can illustrate sentence sense and still not be physically possible.

EXAMPLE: Sally sappy Sam slaps silly

REWRITTEN: Silly Sally slaps sappy Sam. or
              Sappy Sam slaps Sally silly. or
              Sally slaps silly, sappy Sam.

1. Godfrey gashed goofy Gert.
2. baseball the diamond rolled the boy over.
3. a map Myrtle drew floor on the.
4. car the seats on the bars are stacked candy.
5. frog an beautiful into turned prince ugly a.
6. explored Jacques in the Cousteau sea.
7. slippery hair combed his Fonzie slick.

8. breathtaking the view Mt. Rainier from is.
9. the wrong football ran the way with Wesley.
10. pad the blasted spaceship the from launching.
11. green the chili Stooges torpedoed the three.
12. hydrant opened the fire boy the on corner street the.
13. vault robber the inside himself the locked bank.
14. math English passed and Lisa geography.
15. melted the hot sun ice the.

Never Heard Before Sentences

Since you are an expert about the patterns of our language, you hear things you never heard before and understand them. Why? You know how language works. To prove this to you, we have given you totally unique sentences. Some of the sentences will seem ridiculous, and the situations will be impossible. You will understand them, however, because you know patterns of our language.

EXERCISE 3: As a group activity, discuss the meanings of the following sentences. Explain them in your own words.

1. Elephants hardly ever cut lawns, but frequently they lie on their backs and trip low-flying pigeons.
2. Frog-mobiling is forbidden on Lake Poygan from sundown to sunup.
3. Ninety-one percent of the zebra population of South Dakota never tried Wheaties.
4. The smiling clown mopped the kitchen floor while watching "All My Children."
5. Hutch Hundley ate corn grits and quiche while flying in a DC 767 over Canada.
6. Kathy stung the fly while flying a kite made of aluminum.
7. Pizza tastes delicious with peanut butter and jelly spread on top of the anchovies.
8. Billie Bowens billed the bakery for the buttered bread.
9. While watching the Edmonton Oilers on television, Sandra memorized "The Gettysburg Address" in French.
10. Bradley Bear, the only polar bear occupying offices in the "You Betcha Life Insurance Building," usually eats lunch at the zoo.

Special Note: If you did not know English language patterns, you would never be able to understand these ridiculous sentences. In fact, all you would be able to understand is what you have already been taught. Since you're learning new things all the time, you have proven you know language patterns.

Double, Triple, Quadruple Meanings

Sometimes your audience (listener or reader) gets a different meaning from what you say or write than you intended. In your mind the meaning is clear, but, unfortunately, your audience gets a different message.

Study the example sentence, and look at the different meanings:

EXAMPLE: Melva is a light housekeeper.

Meaning One:	Melva does light housework such as dusting.
Meaning Two:	Melva does not weigh very much.
Meaning Three:	Melva works in a lighthouse, and she warns sailors of rocky shores.
Meaning Four:	Melva works in a house light in color.

Think of other meanings.

EXERCISE 4: As a group activity, read the following sentences. See if you can come up with more than one meaning for each one.

1. I saw Boulder Dam on the bus this morning.
2. Baby swallows fly.
3. Flying planes can be dangerous.
4. Butch opened the safe with Miguel.
5. The sisters are ready to serve.
6. I decided on the plane.
7. Watch the screen, and I'll go through it again for you.
8. They fed her dog biscuits.
9. Milking cows can be sloppy.
10. The doctor injected the kid in the bathrobe.
11. Mrs. Claybush admitted shooting her husband from the witness stand during the trial.
12. Ms. Whitmore taught George Washington in the first grade.
13. Albert played baseball with his brother Harry.
14. Herbert washes with Zest. (zest)
15. Kelvin hit the homer with a sore wrist.
16. I fed the lions with my hands.
17. Delbert Daring makes his living by shooting stars.

Special Hint: When you communicate to your audience, make sure your message is clear. Remember, what you say or write might be interpreted differently by your audience. Avoid ambiguous, unclear meanings.

Language Flexibility

Almost every moment of our lives we use language in new, creative ways. Often we are not aware of this. By simply changing the position of a word, we often change its meaning and use.

Here is an example. Baxter Budduck is a multi-talented but restless person. He holds a job for a while. Since he bores quickly, he quits and switches to another job. Presently he works for a circus and **trains seals**. Let's give Baxter another job by changing the position of the "trains" and "seals." Now Baxter **seals trains**. His new job requires Baxter to check box cars to see that there are no leaks.

EXERCISE 5: On a separate sheet of paper, explain Baxter's present job. Then, flip-flop the second and third words. Explain Baxter's new job. Use your imagination. Be creative. (Note: Each explanation is a complete sentence.)

EXAMPLE: Baxter sails ships. Baxter is a sailor.
Baxter ships sails. Baxter is a clerk in a shipping yard and sends out sails.

1. Baxter carts boxes. Baxter _____
   Baxter boxes carts. Baxter _____
2. Baxter paints shelves. Baxter _____
   Baxter shelves paints. Baxter _____
3. Baxter repairs clocks. Baxter _____
   Baxter clocks repairs. Baxter _____
4. Baxter pops bottletops. Baxter _____
   Baxter bottletops pops. Baxter _____
5. Baxter shingles house. Baxter _____
   Baxter houses shingles. Baxter _____

EXERCISE 6: Give our restless worker some other jobs. Explain them as you did for Exercise 5.

Many Uses of a Word

A word can have many different uses in a sentence. It can be used as a noun, a verb, or even an adjective. The only way we know a word's use (function) is by how it interacts with the other words in the sentence. For example, if your teacher asked you to name the part of speech of the word "man," most of you would probably say noun. You might be wrong!

Look at the following sentence. Note the different uses (functions) for the word "man."

Man! Did that **man man** the **man** ship.
  1   2   3   4

1. exclamation or interjection; an expression of wonder, just like the word "Wow!"
2. noun (doer of the action); a person
3. verb (action performed); to operate or control
4. adjective (describes the kind of ship); a man ship might be a ship full of men

EXERCISE 7: As a group activity, discuss the different uses for the bold words in the following sentences.

1. Will the **hound hound** the **hound dog**?
2. The **fired fireman fired** the **fire**.
3. The **eye eyed** the **eyeglasses**.
4. The **watchdog watched** the **watch**.
5. **Can** you open the **can** of **canned** peaches with a **can** opener?
6. The **palmist palmed** the twenty bucks under a **palm** for reading a **palm**.
7. The coach **cut** up the **cut** off man after he **cut** him from the team.
8. The **pickler pickled** the **pickles** picked for **pickling.**
9. **Dusty**, the **duster, dusted** the **dusty duster**.
10. **Bill** paid the **bill** out of his **billed billfold**.

Many Meanings of a Word

In the previous exercise, you saw that words can have many uses (parts of speech) in a sentence. They can also have many meanings or definitions. Discuss the many meanings of the word "floated" in the following sentences:

Floated

1. The pitcher **floated** up a knuckle ball.
2. The boat **floated** on the lake.
3. The balloon **floated** in the sky.
4. The odor **floated** in the locker room

5. The foam **floated** on top of the cold root beer.
6. The bank manager **floated** a loan.

EXERCISE 8: Without changing the use of the following words, make new sentences with new meanings. Do this as a group activity.

Nouns
1. pitch
2. cut
3. call

Verbs
1. fire(d)
2. strike (struck)
3. circle(d)

Some Special Examples

1. The **pitch** was called a ball. (n)
2. The **pitch** on the tree was sticky. (n)
3. The **cut** bled profusely. (n)
4. The **cut** of beef looked tender. (n)
5. I waited for the telephone **call** all night. (n)
6. The **call** by the referee caused my team to lose. (n)
7. The boss **fired** the worker. (v)
8. The starting pistol was **fired** into the air. (v)
9. I'll **strike** the match so we can see. (v)
10. The army will **strike** at dawn. (v)
11. Ron Kittle **circled** the bases. (v)
12. The wagon train **circled** the wagons at night. (v)

EXERCISE 9: Words, then, may have many uses and meanings. As a group activity, change the uses and meanings of the following words.

1. sit
2. push
3. up
4. down
5. run
6. drop

EXAMPLE: cut

1. Leslie is a **cut-up**.
2. Coach Hardnose **cut** Webster from the team.
3. Little Wendy saves **cut-outs**.
4. Sam **cut** the lawn yesterday.
5. Wilbur **cut** class yesterday.
6. Stacey made the **cut** list.

Think of more!

New Verbs

A good writer uses concrete verbs in sentences. These action words make the reader see and feel what the writer sees and feels. Part of the flexibility of our language is that we can create new verbs. Look at the verbs in the following example. Explain what each bold verb means.

EXAMPLE: Professor Wilson **A'ed** the papers, **drawered** her pencils, **shelved** her books, and **deshoed** her feet.

EXERCISE 10: As a group activity, explain what each of the verbs in bold means in the sentences that follow.

1. Calvin **keyed** the garage door.
2. The chef **ovened** the apple pie.
3. Uncle Ziggy **curtained** the windows in the guest house.
4. The mechanic **mufflered** the car in an hour.
5. Kelly **benched** the hammer after using it.
6. Art **iceboxed** the turkey after dinner.
7. Paul **garbaged** the empty boxes.
8. Aggie **desnowed** the sidewalk.
9. Roger **clothespinned** the laundry on a clear, spring day.
10. The Miller family **wintered** in Florida.

EXERCISE 11: Make a list of five object words (nouns). Then use each object word as a verb in an original sentence. Be creative. Use your imagination. Exchange your sentences with a classmate. See if your classmate can understand your "new verbs."

EXAMPLE: wheel

REWRITTEN: Lamont **wheeled** his books into the basement.

EXAMPLE: sardine

REWRITTEN: Billy **sardined** his crackers for a late-night snack.

Creating New Words

Besides creating new verbs out of object words, nouns, you can create new words. Television and radio commercials and newspaper and magazine ads do this all the time. A toilet paper company created the word "stroft" to describe its product. "Stroft" is a combination of "strong" and "soft." Similarly, weather reporters in the Midwest talk about approaching "thorms."

EXERCISE 12: As a group activity, explain the meaning of the words in bold print.

1. Robbie suffers from **sitlessness**.
2. The **heightlessness** of the basement made Lisa feel safe.
3. Morgan **smartlessly unsewed** his pants by bending over too quickly.
4. Uncle Billy praised Christopher for his **flunklessness** last semester.
5. The **chocolateful** pan boiled on the stove.
6. Because Ramos keeps in good shape, he doesn't worry about **quicklessness**.
7. The worried nurse cautioned the old man about his **agefullness**.
8. The **inspectagator** made sure little Jessica had dusted under the bed.
9. **Dancingly** Luke moved down the aisle.
10. Dr. J **skydunkenly** slammed the basketball through the hoop.

EXERCISE 13: Create five of your own words. Use your imagination. Write these words in original sentences. Exchange your new creations with a classmate. See if your classmate can figure out the meanings of your new words.

Word Stretches — Idioms

Words also have meanings that are not found in dictionaries. The meanings are different from what they seem to say. These new meanings are called word stretches or "idioms."

Here is an example:

You'd better **shake a leg**, or you will be late for dinner.

This phrase means that you'd better **hurry**.

Here is another example:

If Mr. Botany finds out that I didn't finish the experiment, I'll be in **hot water**.

What do the words in bold print mean?

EXERCISE 14: As a group activity, discuss the word stretches, idioms, in the following sentences. Some of them might be difficult for you to understand because they are specific to a particular part of the country.

1. The quarterback **threw a bomb** for the touchdown.
2. Carlos **passed the buck.**
3. Ferdinand is **tied to his mother's apron strings.**
4. Barbara is **out in left field.**
5. They sent Orlando to the **funny farm.**
6. Melvin acts like he **belongs in a zoo.**
7. Unable to sit still, Bobby must have **ants in his pants.**
8. Dom's Chevy is a real **lemon.**
9. **Cat got your tongue**?
10. Leo and Larry **got skunked** fishing yesterday.

EXERCISE 15: Make up a list of your own word stretches. Ask your parents, grandparents, or friends for some help. Share your final list with the rest of the class. See if they can figure out the meaning.

UNIT TWO SENTENCE MANIPULATION

STUDENT LEARNING OBJECTIVES

1. The student will break down sentences into kernel ideas.
2. The student will combine kernel ideas.
3. The student will rearrange kernel ideas, placing ideas in key positions in a sentence.
4. The student will subtract unnecessary words from a sentence.
5. The student will expand using the journalistic questions.
6. The student will vary sentence openings and lengths.
7. The student will use a sentence opening sheet.
8. The student will identify verbs in sentences.
9. The student will keep all verbs in the same tense.

A sentence is a collection of ideas glued together. These ideas are called kernel ideas. All sentences, no matter how long, come from kernel ideas. Look at the example sentence:

The stalking leopard chased the galloping zebra into the bush.

The above sentence consists of the following kernel ideas:

*1. There is a leopard.
 2. The leopard is stalking.
 3. The leopard chased.
*4. There is a zebra
 5. The zebra is galloping.
*6. There is a bush.

Every time you break down a sentence into kernel ideas, write the kernels as complete sentences. When necessary, add "There is" or "There are" to write complete sentences, not fragments.

Notice that one sentence combined all the kernel ideas into one complete thought. When we speak, we combine kernel ideas.

Good writers combine kernel ideas when they write. Before you begin to practice combining kernel ideas, first break down some longer sentences into kernels.

EXERCISE 1: On a separate sheet of paper, break down the following sentences into kernel ideas. Write the kernel ideas as complete sentences. Identify the verbs in each sentence.

EXAMPLE: The fireman put out the blaze in the white shingled house.

REWRITTEN: *1. There is a fireman.
  *2. There is a blaze.
   3. The fireman put out the blaze.
  *4. There is a house.
   5. The house is white.
   6. The house is shingled. (verbs: put, is)

1. The young child loved the Cabbage Patch doll.
2. The ballet dancer leaped high into the air.
3. The clown tripped over the broken lamp.
4. Frightened by the storm, Cedric ran into the old, haunted house.
5. Racing down the corridor, Wilma slipped and broke her ankle.
6. The bushy-tailed mongrel slept on the bed.
7. Bold and brave, Chief Red Lobster signaled for the attack.
8. Leaping Lizy sprang and spiked the oncoming serve.
9. Sweating Pepe gripped the seams of the soccer ball.
10. Worried Herman chased the big dog out of the school yard.

MANIPULATORY SKILLS

In the first unit you discovered how much you already know about your language. Now it is time to convert your oral language awareness to writing.

Four sentence manipulatory skills will be taught: combining, rearranging, subtracting, and expanding. They are taught for two reasons. First, you automatically use these skills when you speak. Here is an example. Look at the four sentences below and combine them into one sentence.

1. There is a girl.
2. The girl is small.
3. The girl ran.
4. There is a street.

Spontaneously, you probably said one of the following sentences:

1. The small girl ran into the street.
2. There is a small girl who ran into the street.
3. A girl who is small ran into the street.

The greatest computer in the world, your brain, automatically used all four manipulatory skills.

1. You **combined** four sentences into one.
2. You **rearranged** words, perhaps putting "small" before "girl."
3. You **subtracted** unnecessary words. There were 15 words in the original four sentences. How many words did you use?
4. You **expanded** with words that were not included in the original four sentences. Maybe you used the word "into" or "who."

We teach these four skills to take advantage of what you are already doing.

The second reason you will be taught these skills is the more important, however. There four skills must become part of your writing vocabulary. Here is why.

You must learn how to **combine** kernel ideas, so you can write a variety of sentence structures in your essays.

You must learn how to **rearrange** words, so you can vary your sentence openings. Also, you can learn how to create impact in your writing by positioning words in key places in the sentence.

You must learn how to **subtract**, so you do not clutter your writing with empty words. You will learn how to be concise.

You must learn how to **expand**, so you supply specific and supportive details in your writing.

These skills will be taught by using them. Don't fret if you cannot pick out direct objects or present participles.

Combining Kernel Ideas

The combining of kernel ideas is the beginning of writing. The writer decides which word comes first, second, etc. and decides how many kernel ideas to be combined.

All sentences are constructed of idea words and glue words. Idea words are words that represent thoughts or ideas. Traditionally, they are called nouns, verbs, pronouns, adjectives, adverbs, and interjections. Glue words connect idea words. They are called articles or determiners, conjunctions, and prepositions.

In the following example, the kernel ideas have been combined in several different ways. Notice how the writer changed the form of some words. The writer also expanded, using glue words (conjunctions and prepositions), WH words (relative pronouns), and ING words (present participles or gerunds). Many of the sentences were rearranged so each one begins with a different opening. Identify the verbs in each sentence.

EXAMPLE: Patsy **loves** animals. She **works** at the zoo.

REWRITTEN:
1. **Because** Patsy loves animals, she works at the zoo.
2. Patsy loves animals **since** she works at the zoo.
3. Patsy loves animals, **and** she works at the zoo.
4. Patsy loves animals **and** works at the zoo.
5. **Loving** animals, Patsy works at the zoo.
6. Patsy **is working** at the zoo **because** she loves animals.
7. Patsy, **who** loves animals, works at the zoo.
8. **An animal lover,** Patsy, works at the zoo.
9. **Working** at the zoo is Patsy, an animal lover.
10. **A zoo worker,** Patsy, loves animals.

Before combining kernel sentences, we need a brief review of the comma rules discussed in **Open the Deck**.

COMMA RULE 1 To combine three or more items in a series, place a comma after each item except the final one.

EXAMPLE: Barbara ate fresh potatoes.
Barbara ate salty potatoes.
Barbara ate fried potaotes.

REWRITTEN: Barbara ate **fresh, salty, fried** potatoes.

COMMA RULE 2 To combine two complete sentences using a boys fan word, place a comma before the boys fan (coordinating conjunction) word.

BOYS FAN WORDS: but, or, yet, so, for, and, nor

EXAMPLE: Steve flies airplanes.
Steve rides motorcycles.

REWRITTEN: Steve flies airplanes, **and** and he rides motorcycles.

COMMA RULE 3 To combine two ideas of unequal importance using a glue word (subordinating conjunction), place a comma after the first clause when the glue word begins a sentence. If the glue word is in the middle of the sentence, no comma is necessary.

GLUE WORDS: after, because, although, since, before, etc.

EXAMPLE: Larry plays in a band every night.
Larry earns straight A's.

REWRITTEN: Although Larry plays in a band every night, he still earns straight A's.

COMMA RULE 4 To combine sentences using WH words (relative pronouns), determine if the WH clause is necessary to the meaning of the sentence. If necessary, no commas are needed. If the WH clause adds extra information, not important or necessary to the meaning of the sentence, place commas before and after the WH clause.

WH WORDS: who, whose, whom, which, that

EXAMPLE: There is a house on the corner.
The house on the corner was burglarized.

REWRITTEN: The house **which** is on the corner was burglarized.*

*The information inserted within the sentence is important and necessary to the meaning of the rewritten sentence. It is not necessary to use commas to surround the WH clause.

EXAMPLE: There is a house on the corner.
The house is red.

REWRITTEN: The house, **which** is red, is on the corner.*

*The information inserted within this sentence is not necessary to the meaning of the sentence. Therefore, it is necessary to add the commas around the WH clause.

COMMA RULE 5 When a combined sentence begins with an ING phrase (participle phrase), place a comma after the ING phrase.

EXAMPLE: The house creaks at night.
The house is spooky.

REWRITTEN: Creaking at night, the house is spooky.

EXERCISE 2: Combine the kernel ideas in two or three different ways. Use glue words (subordinating conjunctions and prepositions), WH words (relative pronouns), and ING words (present participles and gerunds). Read your sentences aloud to hear if they are structured correctly. Name the main verb in each combined sentence. Do the first two sets as a group activity. As a help, we have suggested combining words. Refer to the comma rules on the previous page.

1. Maurice loves to browse. He likes Washington Square. (because, who, browsing)
2. The hunter shot the bear. The bear was a fierce grizzly. (since, which)
3. My cat woke my family. It meowed all night. (because, which, waking, or meowing)
4. Snowmobiling is great winter sport. It can be dangerous. (although, which)
5. Shirley was shy. Shirley asked Sheldon to the spring dance.
6. Terry left later than usual. His first class had been postponed.
7. Melanie walked carefully on the ice pond. She heard a slight crack.
8. Wendy enjoys flying a kite. She flies kites on windy days.
9. Dracula led her into the chamber. He held her hand gently.
10. Students dashed out of school. The siren blared.

SPECIAL NOTE: After you have combined each set in two or three different ways, place a star by the best sentence in the set.

EXERCISE 3: Combine the following using glue words, WH words, and ING words. Do the first three as a group activity. Vary your openings with each set. Name the verb in each combined sentence.

EXAMPLE: I walked along the beach. A large dog followed me. It foamed at the mouth.

REWRITTEN: **As** I walked along the beach, a large dog followed me and foamed at the mouth. (glue word)

Foaming at the mouth, a large dog followed me as I walked along the beach. (ING word)

A large dog **which** foamed at the mouth followed me as I walked along the beach. (WH word)

1. Dirk Redfield buckled his holster. He walked over to the cafe. He ordered the quiche of the day.
2. The rapids swirled wildly. Bigsley was shooting the rapids. The canoe disappeared.
3. I took an afternoon snooze. A large wasp awakened me. It circled around my head.
4. Two dogs barked all night. They sat under the porch. They disturbed the Simons family.
5. Some people stayed in their seats. The seats were cushioned. The rock concert was over.
6. Tyrone grabbed the dictionary. He lifted it high into the air. He smacked Tanya on the head.
7. Ginger approached home plate. She gripped the bat tightly. She stared at the pitcher.
8. Sanford turned the corner. He bumped into Sledge Kammer. Sledge Kammer was the school bully.
9. The fans sobbed. They smashed their programs to the floor. They couldn't believe the final score.
10. The raging furnace exploded. It sent up clouds of smoke. The smoke was black and billowing.
11. The truck screeched to a halt. Darsey Dingfield bolted out of the driver's seat. Darsey Dingfield ran to the accident.
12. The jet fighter approached the flight deck. Sherman Smoot cut the engine. The plane bounced to a safe landing.
13. Erica sat at her desk. She took a deep breath. She began her semester test.
14. Little Webster laughed. He was delighted by Ronald McDonald. Ronald McDonald drove a McDonald Burgermobile.
15. Marcie the mechanic opened the hood. She removed the air filter. She released the stuck choke.

SPECIAL NOTE: After you have combined each set in two or three different ways, place a star by the one sentence in each set which you like best.

Rearranging Kernel Ideas

As you practice combining kernel ideas, you also rearranged words in different positions. If you read some of your sentences aloud, you probably noticed that by moving words or phrases to different positions, you created a different emphasis. We like to call this creating a desired **IMPACT** upon your reader.

As a writer, you must be aware of the key positions in a sentence.

In this way if you want to create a desired impact, emphasis, you can rearrange the words in the sentence.

Read the following three sentences. Pick out the one sentence that emphasizes the word "loudly" the most.

A. The cat meowed **loudly** all night long.
B. All night long the cat meowed **loudly**.
C. **Loudly** the cat meowed all night long.

You probably selected B or C. In B, "loudly" is the last word in the sentence. The writer positioned "loudly" last to build up suspense. It also leaves the reader with a lasting impression. In C, the writer tells the reader exactly what is to be emphasized. In A, "loudly" gets lost in the middle of the sentence. Consequently, to emphasize something, put it either at the beginning or the end of a sentence.

There is another reason why you need to practice the skill of rearranging. A bad habit some students get into while writing is they begin each sentence with the same opening. Their sentences begin with "The," "The," "The;" "I," "I," "I;" "And then," "And then," "And then," etc. When you spot these repetitious openings in your own writing, rearrange. The Sentence Opening Sheet, which will be introduced later in this unit, will be a big help for you.

EXERCISE 4: Rearrange the following sentences to emphasize a word or phrase that is important to you. First, pick out the idea you want to emphasize. Then rearrange it in a position of importance (first or last). Then name the main verb in each sentence. Do the first three as a group activity. In these sentences, the main ideas have been highlighted for you.

1. Little Robin inched her way **courageously** to the haunted house on a stormy night.
2. I waited **alone** for twenty minutes.
3. Ms. Pumpkin stopped **abruptly** and stared at Herman.
4. Dr. I. Pullem reached into Aileen's mouth and forcefully grasped her wisdom tooth with his pliers.
5. Nothing is more beautiful to me than a quiet evening in Wisconsin.
6. As lightning streaked across the sky, Jennifer and Samantha screamed and hid under the bed.
7. It pleased Uncle Dick to eat the pickled herring from my refrigerator.

8. Mr. Samuel Puzatero screamed with delight when he found the missing Brinks money bag.
9. I felt like a millionaire as I boarded the ship for Transylvania.
10. Sliding down the banister in the old people's home, Maggie McDunna ripped her bloomers.

SPECIAL NOTE: Another way to create **IMPACT** is to rearrange words so you put them out of their normal order. Adjectives normally come before the word they modify. Notice the difference in emphasis by rearranging the bold words. Name the main verb in each rewritten sentence.

EXAMPLE: A **tall, dark** stranger crept up the stairs.

REWRITTEN: A stranger, **tall and dark**, crept up the stairs.

After reading the two sentences aloud, can you hear the difference in **IMPACT** in the two sentences?

EXERCISE 5: Rearrange the following sentences. Put the bold words in an **unusual** position for emphasis. Underline the main verb in your rewritten sentence.

1. The **spacious** and **bright** room will make an ideal place for a workshop.
2. **Scott John** is an excellent athlete and a hard working student.
3. A **dark** and **heavy** cloud moved across the lake.
4. I could not accept **Mildred's insult.**
5. Aggie is **funny** and **friendly**, and she is the life of the party.

Subtracting Kernel Ideas

Have you ever counted your words as you were writing a composition? Maybe your teacher assigned you 150 or 250 words, and you wanted to see if you had enough.

If you didn't "hit" the assigned number, maybe you added words to fill up space. You might have added an idea not necessary to your composition. You might even have repeated the same idea in different words. Quantity, not quality, was your concern. Filling a composition with unnecessary words is a common student problem. A simple remedy is to subtract. Read the following student sentence. The unnecessary words have been printed in bold.

EXAMPLE: The man **who was** chained to the chair broke loose with a lunge **which was** mighty.

Notice how the empty words have been subtracted.

REWRITTEN: The man chained to the chair broke loose with a mighty lunge.

You might even want to rearrange this sentence to create a different emphasis, **IMPACT.**

REWRITTEN: With a mighty lunge the man chained to the chair broke loose.

Try another example.

EXAMPLE: I cleaned up the basement, which was filthy, and which is a job that I hate to do.

Notice how the empty words have been subtracted in the revised sentence.

REWRITTEN: I cleaned the filthy basement even though I hate the job.

EXERCISE 6: Rewrite the following sentences subtracting the unnecessary words or repeated ideas. Identify the main verb in each rewritten sentence. Do the first two as a group activity.

NOTE: Avoid YUK (snow job) in writing. Read the sentences aloud. This helps the writer to hear the unnecessary words and ideas.

1. We thought in our minds how we might descend to the bottom of the canyon, which is huge and big.
2. The boy who is small and who is floating in the lake was bitten by a snake, which is slimy.
3. The old watch that I bought at the pawn shop is an old Timex watch, a watch with good features.
4. The newspaper truck, which is a **New York Times** truck, was skidding down Wall Street and smashed into a car, which was a police car.
5. On Sunday morning, which was really hot, Risnosnick Oblenglobben Fuffarachack Aruttenputtnavich was strolling down a street, which is made of cobblestone.
6. Little Victoria, who is small, walked along the road, and it was a nice day, and she was picking up aluminum cans.

7. Michael Jackson, who once was a childhood star from Gary, Indiana, keeps busy by recording albums, and he also keeps busy by doing television commercials.
8. In my imagination I imagine while I am dreaming that I won the lottery, which is worth $12,000,000.
9. The fire which was blazing caused the house made of wood to burn to the ground.
10. I like to play baseball, and I like to eat apple pie, and I like to listen to old records of Elvis Presley, and these are my hobbies.
11. The book was boring, and I was bored reading it because it was so dull.
12. One example of that trait is that the boy named Walter is always daydreaming.
13. Because of the fact that it was foggy outside, the two cars collided.
14. The reason that the city of Seattle is an exciting city is that it offers many exciting activities for those people who say they enjoy the out of doors.
15. I enjoy playing computer games, and I enjoy watching horror movies.

Expanding Kernel Ideas

Have you ever sat at your desk and began to write a composition, but you couldn't think of what to write? Or maybe your teacher returned a composition back to you and you noticed the comment "Be specific" written all over. Those are common student problems. The fourth manipulatory skill, **expanding**, should help you solve this problem.

As a writer, you must make sure your audience understands what you are communicating. Expanding your kernel ideas with journalistic questions will help. Journalists call them the five w's and an h.

who
what
when
where
why
how

Look at the following sentence:

EXAMPLE: The uncle bought a gift for his niece.

You didn't know **who** the uncle and niece were, **what** the gift was, or **why** the uncle bought it.

Here's an expanded sentence with the who, what, and why questions answered.

REWRITTEN: Uncle Herb bought Jessica a tic-tac-toe game for her fourth birthday.

EXERCISE 7: Expand the following sentences by answering the given journalistic questions. Identify the main verbs in each expanded sentence. Do the first two as a group activity.

1. The (what kind) man hobbled (how) toward the emergency room. (why)
2. (when) The lights flickered on and off, and the (what kind) children hid.
3. (how) The (what kind) umpire shouted, "Play ball!"
4. Bobbi flew her (what kind) kite. (where)
5. Chester fixed the flat tire and (how) threw the jack. (where)
6. The (what kind) wind blew (where) and bent Ray's boat lift.
7. The (what kind) bird chirped. (how) (why)
8. Melvin (how) ate the (what kind) pizza and (how) complimented the (what kind) chef.
9. Cynthia paused (how) and walked (how) from the stage. (why)
10. My sister (how) picked up the broken glass and threw it. (where)

EXERCISE 8: Expand the following sentences by answering the given journalistic questions. Identify the main verbs in each expanded sentence. Do the first two as a group activity.

1. The teacher talked about student behavior. What teacher? What kind of student behavior? Where?
2. The little boy is going to have a good time. Who is the little boy? Why is he going to have a good time?
3. The game was exciting. What kind of game? Where was the game played? Why was it exciting?
4. The dog hates being chained. What kind of dog? Why does he hate being chained?
5. Robert cleaned James' room. When did Robert clean the room? What kind of room does James have? Why did Robert clean it?
6. The cat eyed the bird. What kind of cat? How did the cat eye the bird?
7. The robber peeked into the window. When did the robber peek into the window? How did he peek?

8. The bee stung the baby. What kind of bee? How did it sting the baby? What did the baby do?
9. People complained about the increase in prices. Who are the people complaining? What did they complain about?
10. The child loves practice. Who is the child? What type of practice does he love? Why does he love practice?

EXERCISE 9: It is important to combine the skills just learned and practiced. As a group activity, choose two or three rewritten sentences from each of the two previous exercises and rearrange the sentences to change the **IMPACT.**

EXERCISE 10: Expand the kernel ideas by answering all the journalistic questions. However, as you begin to combine the ideas, use the main kernel, plus three of your responses. If you use all the questions, you might write some long, awkward sentences. Underline the main verb in the written sentence.

EXAMPLE: basking in the sun

who . . . . Bobbi Mitchell
what . . . . already answered (basking in the sun)
when . . . . during the heat of the summer
where . . . . on Lake Shasta
why . . . . to get a tan
how . . . . sleepily

REWRITTEN: During the heat of the summer at Lake Shasta, Bobbi Mitchell sleepily **basked** in the sun to get a tan.

By rearranging the words in your combined sentence, you can create a different **IMPACT.** What did the writer stress in the following sentence?

REWRITTEN: To get a summer tan, Bobbi Mitchell **basked** in the sun on a hot summer day on Lake Shasta.

SPECIAL NOTE: Once you write your first expanded sentence, rearrange it to stress another kernel idea. Vary your openings, underline the main verb in each sentence, and mark the sentence which sounds best in each set.

1. talks on the C.B.
2. Wilbur crashed
3. hissing loudly
4. slips on the street
5. Meg volleys
6. screaming aloud

7. arguing with . . .
8. dancing
9. while babysitting
10. allowance money
11. before school
12. making the rally squad
13. during the tornado
14. Michael Jackson
15. science experiment
16. scoring the winning point
17. Olympics
18. in the airplane
19. on the first day of school
20. painfully

Putting It All Together
STAGE ONE: PREWRITING

Now it is the time to use all four skills in writing a paragraph. This requires some planning:

1. Read the paragraph three or four times aloud to see if you understand the content.
2. Decide which sentences can be combined to form more complicated and interesting sentences.
3. Combine these grouped sentences. You may use glue words (subordinating conjunctions and prepositions), WH words (relative pronouns), and ING words (present participles or gerunds).

Before you begin to work on one of the models, your teacher might demonstrate one as a group activity.

Unofficial Party

1. Irving A. Ghast peered out of the window. 2. He saw his parents. 3. He was shocked. 4. He was having an unofficial party. 5. He regained his "cool." 6. He began cleaning up. 7. He did it quickly. 8. He told the guests to leave. 9. They left hurriedly. 10. Irving was frightened. 11. He rearranged the furniture. 12. He saw a soda stain. 13. It was on the couch. 14. There was a pillow. 15. He placed it on the stain. 16. There was a sink. 17. Hastily he put the dishes in it. 18. He broke one. 19. He cleaned up the fragments quickly. 20. Everything looked normal. 21. The pile of garbage was the only exception. 22. Irving opened the door. 23. His parents stood in the doorway. 24. They had angry faces.

Alone in the Dark House

1. It was night. 2. Joan was alone. 3. Her mother had left. 4. She was in the house. 5. The house was huge and dark colored. 6.

The night was scary. 7. Joan walked over to the television. 8. She turned it on. 9. It was in the living room. 10. She watched. 11. It became boring and tiring. 12. She stood up. 13. She walked over to the television set. 14. She was going to turn it off. 15. She noticed a horror show had come on. 16. Joan sat back down. 17. Time passed. 18. The show became exciting and interesting. 19. She heard a strange noise. 20. Joan saw a strange figure. 21. The figure was on the wall. 22. The figure made a weird noise. 23. She wanted to scream. 24. She didn't. 25. She sat still and quiet. 26. The figure came closer. 27. She felt a hugging and a pulling at her neck. 28. This was sudden. 29. She screamed. 30. Her mother returned to the house. 31. Her mother ran into the room. 32. Joan woke up. 33. She jumped up. 34. Her mother reassured her. 35. She only had a bad dream. 36. She promised not to watch another horror movie alone.

Date

1. It was our fifth date. 2. I wanted to hold Priscilla's hand. 3. I figured it was the least I would do. 4. There was a movie. 5. It was technicolored. 6. Her eyes stayed glued to it. 7. I battled a case of hiccups. 8. It was a severe case. 9. My throat was unusually dry. 10. I cleared it. 11. I cleared it three or four times. 12. Priscilla gave me a look. 13. It was a questioning look. 14. I was nervous. 15. I crumpled a candy box. 16. Priscilla was calm. 17. She munched popcorn. 18. I fidgeted with my hands. 19. I was trying to decide. 20. I didn't know which hand to reach out with. 21. She had a lace sleeve on her dress. 22. I dropped my hand. 23. It dropped jerkily. 24. It fell on her lace sleeve. 25. She turned to me. 26. She said to me. 27. She said that the picture was over. 28. She said that we should go home.

STAGE TWO: WRITING THE FIRST DRAFT

Now that you have decided upon which sentences can be grouped, combine them using glue words, WH words, and ING words. As you begin to write, occasionally stop to reread what you have written. You might want to rearrange a sentence or use a different opening. Write your sentences on every other line and number your sentences.

Now begin writing your first draft.

STAGE THREE: REWRITING

With your first draft finished, read your paragraph through carefully and circle all verbs. Then, fill out a Sentence Opening Sheet (SOS). This SOS or "help sheet" will assist you in locating errors on your first draft.

The SOS sheet has four columns. A sketchy model follows:

First Four Words	Special	Verbs	# of words per sentence
1. Irving peering out the	past	saw	7

Column One   **First Four Words**

Write down the first four words of each sentence. This enables you to see if your sentences begin with the same openings. If they do, you need to apply the skills of combination and rearrangement.

Also, if your sentences begin with a glue word (subordinating conjunction), read that sentence to see if it is a fragment. A good way to check for fragments in paragraphs is to read the paper backwards one sentence at a time. You begin with your last sentence and stop. Does it make sense? This reading aloud helps you to hear incomplete thoughts.

EXAMPLE: 9. The fishermen stayed in the cabin. 10. Because the wind blew so fiercely.

Sentence 10 is a fragment. By reading forward, you might not hear the fragment. Your mind combined sentences 9 and 10. However, by reading one sentence at a time backwards and pausing after each sentence, you could hear the fragment.

Column Two   **Special**

This column can be used for a variety of items. If your teacher wanted you to emphasize use of glue words, you would list each glue word used in the paragraph.

For this paragraph, verb tense consistency is important. Therefore, we will use the special column to record the tense of the verbs listed in column three. The best tense for this paragraph is PAST tense.

Column Three   **Verbs**

Read each sentence carefully. Write the main verbs from each sentence in the verb column. Each main verb is written on its own line.

This enables you to see if you used the same verb over and over again. (VP-Verb Power) How about "got," "got,", or "is," "is," or "are," etc. Remember: ING words are not verbs unless they have a BE verb helper. Also to **+** a verb (infinitive phrase) does not need to be listed in the verb column.

EXAMPLE: 9. The fisherman stayed in the cabin.

The word "stayed" is listed in column three, and "past" is written in column two for the tense.

Column Four   **Number of Words Per Sentence**

Count the number of words you used in each sentence. This helps you identify two things. First, if your sentences are all the same length, you might need to combine and/or rearrange them. Second, if you included too many words in a sentence, 20 for example, you should reread it to make sure it is not a run-on.

NAME _____ PERIOD _____

SENTENCE OPENINGS (First Four Words)	SPECIAL	VERBS	# OF WORDS PER SENTENCE

FIRST DRAFT FINISHED

Now fill out a Sentence Opening Sheet for your first draft. One or two of you might volunteer your SOS sheet for an overhead projector transparency. The class could study them as a model to analyze their own SOS sheets. Your teacher might even have you exchange SOS sheets. Here are some questions to use in checking over each column:

Column One   **First Four Words**

1. Do the sentences begin with the same openings?
2. Do any sentences need to be combined and/or rearranged to make them more interesting?
3. Do any sentences begin with a glue word making them perhaps fragments?

Column Two   **Special**

1. Are all my verbs in the same tense? (PAST)

Column Three   **Verbs**

1. Did I use the same verbs over and over again?
2. Could I use more specific verbs to make the sentence more lively?

Column Four   **Number of Words Per Sentence**

1. Are all my sentences the same length?
2. Can I combine some of my sentences to make them more interesting?
3. Are any of my longer sentences run-ons?

ANTICIPATED FIRST DRAFT COMPOSITION ERRORS

After you have studied your Sentence Opening Sheet, you will want to make corrections of your first draft. By skipping lines on your first draft, you have allowed yourself space to make those necessary corrections.

Also, student first draft errors have been included. You can see if similar mistakes appear on your first draft. There are three types of mistakes for each model paragraph: fragments, run-ons, and verb tense consistency.

EXAMPLE: Irving A. Ghast **peers**¹ out the window he **saw**² his parents he **was shocked**.³

1. VT   Verb tense consistency
2. RO   Run-on sentence
3. RO   Run-on sentence

SPECIAL RUN-ON HINT

Here are four ways to correct run-on sentences:

1. Use a period as an end punctuation mark. Capitalize the first word of the second sentence.

    Irving A. Ghast peered out the **window, and** he saw his **parents. He was shocked.**

2. Use a comma plus a boys fan (coordinating conjunction).

    Irving A. Ghast peered out the **window, and** he saw his **parents. He** was shocked.

3. Use a semicolon if the two sentences are closely related in meaning.

    Irving A. Ghast peered out the **window; he saw** his **parents. He was** shocked.

4. Rewrite the sentence using glue words, WH words, or ING words.

When Irving A. Ghast peered out the window, he saw his parents, **which** shocked him.

Peering out the window, Irving A. Ghast saw his parents, **which** shocked him.

EXERCISE 11: Correct the errors in the following sentences. Use the skills of combination, rearrangement, subtraction, and expansion. First, identify the error. Then rewrite the corrected sentence on a separate sheet of paper.

Unofficial Party

1. As Irving peered out of the window. He saw his parents he was in a state of shock because he was having an unofficial party.
2. His parents standing in the doorway with angry faces.
3. He began cleaning up the house quickly he tells his guests to leave.
4. Seeing a soda stain on the couch.
5. Because he was frightened. Irving tells his guests to leave.

Alone in the Dark

1. Since Joan was alone in the house. She turned on the television.
2. Noticing a horror show on the tv. Joan sat down.
3. Joan sees a figure on the wall the figure made weird noises.
4. Joan's mother was frightened by the scream she came running into the house.
5. As Joan sat quiet and still. The figure comes closer it begins hugging and pulling at her neck.

Date

1. On our fifth date I wanted to hold Priscilla's hand I figure it was the least I could do.
2. Fidgeting with my hands. I try to decide which hand to reach out with.
3. As Priscilla gave me a questioning look. I nervously crumble a candy box and uncrumble it.
4. I battle a severe case of hiccups my throat was extremely dry.
5. While she was munching on the popcorn. I fidget with my hands.

FINAL DRAFT

In rewriting your paper, you should correct all the mistakes from the first draft. The Sentence Opening Sheet and anticipated errors should have helped you spot some of these mistakes. Try to make your final draft error free. Besides your reading your own paper aloud, have a proofreading partner read your paper. Quite often this will help you hear mistakes which you otherwise might have missed. Here are some final questions to ask yourself as you reread your final draft:

1. Have I used the four sentence writing skills?
2. Did I vary my sentence openings?
3. Do I have any fragments because of glue word openings?
4. Are all my verbs in the PAST tense?
5. Do I have any run-ons because of overly long sentences?
6. Do I have a variety of sentence lengths.?

UNIT THREE CONTROLLING IDEA

STUDENT LEARNING OBJECTIVES

1. The student will identify the subject and key words in a controlling idea.
2. The student will list ideas that support the subject and key words in a controlling idea.
3. The student will rewrite poorly written controlling ideas.
4. The student will write a controlling idea that contains a subject and key words.

A paragraph is a group of sentences centering in on one main idea. Often this main idea is stated in one sentence of the paragraph. We call the sentence which contains the main idea the controlling idea.

A controlling idea is a contract between the writer and the reader. It contains two things. First, it names the subject or topic of the paragraph. Second, it gives key words that tell the writer's opinion or ideas about the subject. These key words give the paragraph a sense of direction.

The controlling idea should contain only one subject. It should not contain more ideas than what can be written about in one paragraph. In the following student controlling idea, the subject and key words have been identified.

    Snowmobiling on **Lake Poygan** is a **dangerous activity.**
      subject   key words   key words

The subject is "snowmobiling." The key words that limit the paragraph's direction are "Lake Poygan" and "dangerous activity." In other words, this paragraph can only point out the dangers of snowmobiling on Lake Poygan. The writer's opinion is expressed in the key words.

Here is another student controlling idea:

Learning how to use a computer is a lot easier than most people think.

The subject is "using a computer." The writer's opinion is that it is "a lot easier than most people think." In order to write a well-organized essay for this controlling idea, CI, the writer would have to present us with a step-by-step lesson showing us that computer use is not difficult to learn.

Read the following student composition. The controlling idea has been highlighted. Notice how each idea that follows the CI supports the subject and key words.

Christmas Downtown

Gazing out of the frosted department store window, my eyes capture all the colorful and hectic sights that accompany the Christmas holiday. Stationed at a busy street corner, a Salvation Army Santa Claus shouts a merry "HO, HO, HO" to a passer-by who drops a handful of loose change into a red bucket. Bustling shoppers carrying armloads of packages weave their way through a human maze from department store to department store. Adding to the frantic movement of late-coming shoppers, honking-horn buses, taxies and cars snake their way down icy, snowpacked streets. Large red and white candy canes, holly green wreaths, golden streamers hanging down lamp posts, and trees beautifully decorated with flickering lights turn an ordinary downtown into a breathtaking Christmas wonderland. Then, as if the massive gray clouds in the twilight sky can read my mind, fluffy, white snowflakes begin to drift lazily to the ground, putting the final touch on a vivid and busy scene — Christmas downtown.

In the above composition, the subject of the controlling idea is "Christmas downtown," and the key words are "colorful and hectic sights." All the remaining ideas in the paper prove the key words. The ideas the writer used proved that Christmas downtown is a great place to see colorful and hectic sights.

CONTROLLING IDEA: Gazing out to the frosted department store window, my eyes capture all the colorful and hectic sights that accompany the Christmas holiday.

SUBJECT:
CHRISTMAS DOWNTOWN

KEY WORDS:
COLORFUL AND HECTIC SIGHTS

A composition must be like a perfect circle with every idea contributing to the oneness and unity of the paper.

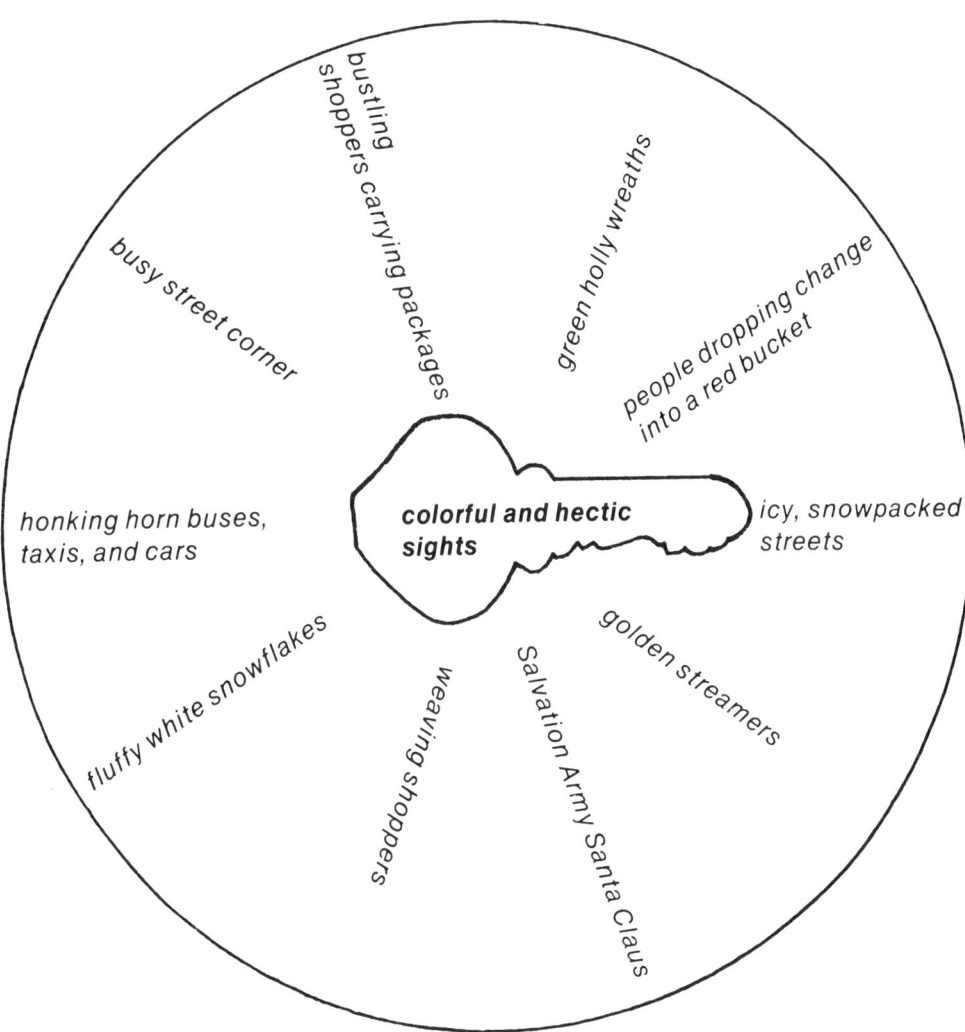

Notice how each spoke of the circle proves the key words in the controlling idea. In order for a composition to be unified, every idea must prove the key words. If, for example, one of the spokes read "ice skating on the slick pond," this statement would not prove the key words and would have to be subtracted from the paper.

Being an Audience

Good writers write with a specific purpose to a specific audience. Before you begin to write your own controlling ideas, you first must be the audience.

EXERCISE 1: Identify the subject and key words in each controlling idea. If you have any difficulty selecting the subject and key words, think of reasons, facts, ideas and examples that would prove the words. It is the key words that will create interest in the audience. Do the first three as a group activity.

1. Vacationers to the Olympic Stadium will long remember the delicious smells carried about by vendors.
2. An audience at a Styx concert wears a variety of clothes.
3. For me, a trip to the zoo is a big bore.
4. To avoid serious accidents, a boater must know the safety regulations in boating.
5. A feeling of happiness swept over Poynter's locker room after their championship win over Evergreen.
6. The tastes in music differ greatly in the Schwartz family.
7. Our trip to the World's Fair in New Orleans was the highlight of my summer vacation.
8. To be a good volleyball player, a person must have certain skills.
9. I get upset when I have to babysit for the Munchko twins.
10. My brother Clarence is the sloppiest person I know.
11. Quarterbacking a football team takes more brains than brawn.
12. Using a microscope is easy if one follows a few easy steps.
13. Learning how to drive a stick-shift automobile can be mastered after a few short lessons.
14. The poems of Edgar Allen Poe shouldn't be read alone on a stormy night.
15. A skiing vacation at Timberline Lodge combines history and majesty.

List Making

To be a good writer, you must be a good thinker. Since each paragraph centers on one controlling idea, all the ideas that follow must support that one idea. To do this, you must think about the topic and key words. Then you must list specific details and examples that support those words. That is what you will practice now.

Look at the first sentence in the previous exercise:

CONTROLLING IDEA: Vacationers to Olympic Stadium will long remember the delicious smells carried about by the vendors.

The topic: smells

The key words: delicious, Olympic Stadium, and vendors

In order to prove this controlling idea, the writer needs to list the delicious smell that the vendors carried about in Olympic Stadium.

Smells		**Specific Ideas**
1. popcorn	How did it smell?	aroma of freshly popped popcorn
2. hot dogs	How did they smell?	plump, juicy, sizzling hot dogs
3. pop	How did it smell?	sweet, sugary smell of ice cold Pepsi
4. pizza	How did it smell?	tangy, spicy pizza cuts sweet
5. cotton candy	How did it smell?	sweet fragrance of fluffy, pink cotton candy
6. fans	How did they smell?	cheering, screaming fans chasing a foul ball
7. cigar	How did it smell?	odor of cigar-smoking men

Do all of the above ideas support the topic and key words of the controlling idea? Which ones do not? Why?

EXERCISE 2: Brainstorm as many ideas as you can as a class for controlling idea 2 in Exercise 1. Do they all fit? Then, work on some of the other controlling ideas from Exercise 1. You might want to exchange lists with a classmate, or your teacher might want to place lists on overhead transparencies for class discussion.

Rewriting Poorly Written Controlling Ideas

Sometimes controlling ideas lack a sense of purpose or direction. The writer includes more than one subject or makes the subject so general that it could not be developed in one paragraph. Or, the controlling idea is nothing more than a direct statement of fact which leaves nothing more to say in the paragraph. In other words, the writer's opinion or ideas about the subject is not clear. The audience is left in confusion.

Here is an example of a poorly written controlling idea:

Japanese automobiles are far superior to American-made cars.

This controlling idea tries to cover too broad of an area.

Here is another example of a poorly written controlling idea:

The decline in attendance in baseball is bad.

The above CI is too general. The reader doesn't know what the word "bad" means.

Here is an example of that same CI rewritten to make it more specific:

The decline in attendance at the Minnesota Twins baseball games has caused problems for businesses in the surrounding area.

The subject is now limited to Minnesota Twins. The key words identify the writer's opinion. To prove this CI, the writer would have to list specific examples from businesses in the surrounding area.

Here is an example of a "so what" type of controlling idea:

Peanut butter and jelly sandwiches taste good.

This is a poorly written CI. It is a direct statement of fact. What would the writer have to prove here? What audience would want to read an entire paragraph about this CI?

Here is the same CI rewritten:

By following my directions, making a peanut butter and jelly sandwich will be a simple task.

EXERCISE 3: Rewrite the following poorly written controlling ideas. First, discuss what is wrong with each one of them. Then rewrite each CI making it more specific. Do the first two as a group activity. Some of your rewritten CI's may be put on overhead projector transparencies for class discussion purposes.

1. Cable television has been installed in most Canadian homes.
2. I ate a half gallon of chocolate ice cream for dessert last night.
3. Sports require more brains than brawn.
4. Teachers give homework on the weekends.
5. In a typical winter there is plenty of snow in the Northeast.
6. Students have fun on their summer vacation during the summer.
7. Exercise helps all kinds of people for many reasons.
8. I take computer classes in school.

9. A convertible is a nice looking car.
10. People from the Midwest are moving to the Sun Belt.
11. The causes of the Civil War are too numerous to mention.
12. Television commercials are funny.
13. Living in a large city has many advantages than living in a small city.
14. Baseball is a difficult sport to play.
15. I have many pleasant memories of my early childhood from age three to seven.

Writing Your Own Controlling Ideas

The previous exercises have dealt with student-written controlling ideas that have been given to you. Now it is time for you to begin writing your own controlling ideas.

Your controlling ideas should contain two items. First, the subject should be specific. Second, key words should tell the reader your opinion or ideas about the subject.

EXERCISE 4: Write controlling ideas for the following subjects. First, funnel the general subject to more specific ones. Second, combine your ideas and include key words that state your opinion or ideas. Do two or three as a group activity.

HINT: Remember when we expanded vague sentences using the six journalistic questions? See page 21 to review.

EXAMPLE:
General Subject............ school spirit
Specific School............. Thornton High School
Specific Event.............. basketball game against Thornwood
Specific Group .... fans, varsity football players sitting together
Specific Action............. leading cheers

CONTROLLING IDEA:
The varsity football team's cheers inspired the basketball victory over Thornwood.

EXAMPLE:
General Subject............ politics
Specific Person............. Mayor Cheatham

Specific Place .... Fort Wade, Idaho
Specific Action .... hired relatives and friends

CONTROLLING IDEA: By hiring his relatives and friends, Mayor Cheatham abused the power of his office.

1. foods
2. clothing
3. vacation trips
4. computers
5. horror movies
6. teachers
7. cooking
8. sports
9. English papers
10. pep rallies
11. parties
12. hair styles
13. generation gap
14. arguments
15. biking
16. gymnastics
17. apartment living
18. gun control
19. July 4th
20. girlfriends / boyfriends
21. homework
22. TV programs
23. rock groups
24. surfing
25. Olympics
26. school rules
27. violence on TV
28. gangs
29. babysitting
30. parents / grandparents

SUPPLEMENTAL EXERCISES: To ensure all students can write well-formed controlling ideas, one or more of the following exercises can be employed.

1. Duplicate student controlling ideas from Exercise 4 on overhead transparencies for class discussion.

2. Have students practice rearrangement with a well-written controlling idea. Then have students choose the CI with the most IMPACT on the reader.

3. Have the class brainstorm controlling ideas for one set of specific details. Then choose the CI with the most IMPACT.

4. Have students choose their two best CI from Exercise 4 and write them on the blackboard. Then as a class, examine and discuss them. Point out subject and key words. Then decide how each CI could be developed into a paragraph.

UNIT FOUR   HOW TO DO PAPER

Since we are often asked to explain something or to give directions, we should learn how to do this correctly. The purpose of this assignment, then, is to explain how to do something to an audience unfamiliar with the process.

STAGE ONE: PREWRITING

Student Learning Objectives

1. The student will state the subject in the controlling idea.
2. The student will organize the ideas in a step-by-step sequence without any gaps. (chronological)
3. The student will supply specific information with each idea.
4. The student will link ideas using glue words.
5. The student will conclude the process with a clincher sentence and/or comment on the completed process.
6. The student will use the command form of the verb.

Helpful Drills

In writing the paper, you should state all steps in the correct order. Occasionally students will skip a step when they write about a topic they are very familiar with. They do not even realize they are doing this because they are so close to the topic. This missing step is called a gap. Before you select a topic, practice the following exercise.

EXERCISE 1: A student was writing a paper on how to cut a lawn and listed over twenty steps on the think sheet. Arrange the steps in proper order. Subtract any unnecessary steps. If you notice a gap, expand with the necessary step. (**NOTE:** There may be differences in the final order.)

1. **Open** a can of cold Pepsi.
2. **Clean** the mower.
3. **Take** the mower out of the garage.
4. **Put** the control on start.
5. **Pull** the cord.
6. **Regulate** the gas.
7. **Find** a seat under some quiet, shade tree.
8. **Check** the oil level on the motor.
9. **Check** the gas level.
10. **Empty** the grass collection bag.

11. **Wheel** the mower to the lawn.
12. **Put** the mower back in the garage.
13. **Chase** the stray dog out of the bushes.
14. **Guide** the mower over the lawn.
15. **Put** the grass collection bag back on the mower.
16. **Hire** some "sucker" to cut the lawn for you.
17. **Turn** on the radio in the garage to WPUX.
18. **Turn** off the mower.
19. **Check** the lawn for rocks, bottles, and dog "surprises."
20. **Go** play softball with kids on the corner.
21. **Set** the cutting height of the mower.
22. **Overlap** over the last cut as you go back and forth.
23. **Call** up Stanley and see if he'll bring his fly swatter.

Subject

Select a subject you are familiar with. This subject should come from something you have done at home, in school, in the garage, or on the playfield, etc. It should be something you have done again and again. Maybe you are an expert at patching a bicycle tire, baking chocolate chip cookies, quieting down a crying baby, stealing second base in baseball, or setting up a lab experiment in science class. The choice is yours. Here are some suggested topics:

1. How to bake a banana cake, etc.
2. How to make chocolate brownies
3. How to make a taco
4. How to make egg salad
5. How to pitch a tent
6. How to prepare for a camping trip
7. How to fillet a fish
8. How to clean a rifle
9. How to break dance
10. How to telephone someone in a foreign country
11. How to bunt a baseball
12. How to serve a tennis ball
13. How to shoot a free throw
14. How to hook up a dog sled
15. How to hatch an egg (science experiment)
16. How to wash a car, motorcycle, airplane, etc.
17. How to sew a button on a shirt
18. How to tie a shoe lace
19. How to set up a video recorder
20. How to get from your home to school by naming landmarks, not streets

These are just suggested topics. Choose something else if these do not appeal to you.

Once you select a topic, mentally brainstorm all the steps that are needed to complete this task. Think!!

Controlling Idea

Since your reader should know your topic immediately, your first sentence should serve as your controlling idea for this paper. Let your audience know what your composition is all about. Here are some sample student controlling ideas:

1. Anyone can learn how to make a mouth-watering banana split by following these simple directions.
2. Developing film is not as difficult as most people think.
3. Giving a horse a bath requires following a simple procedure.

Organizing the Paper

Your paper should be organized in a step-by-step sequence without any gaps. You must include all the information, including materials which are necessary. After you have selected your subject, start thinking about your process. Visualize everything that you do. Here are some questions to think about:

1. What materials are needed to complete this process?
2. What is the first thing I do? How do I do it?
3. What is the second? Third? etc.

Gluing Ideas Together

In writing this paper each idea must lead to the next. You ensure this by following a definite time sequence. You should also use glue words to link steps in your process. The following glue words will help glue your ideas together:

GLUE WORDS: first, second, third, finally, thus, next, furthermore, in addition, again, then, now, gradually

Can you think of other glue words that might be used?

Ending

A paper should never end when you hit the magic number of words assigned. As a good writer, you should plan your ending so it flows naturally out of your paper's development. This "How to Do" paper may end with the logical last step, or you can comment on your finished process. Here are some sample student endings to process papers:

1. Finally, hang the negatives in a dust-free room and let them dry. If these steps have all been done correctly, the negatives will be clean and clear.
2. If you follow these directions carefully, your mouth will enjoy the most delicious homemade pizza ever made.

Command Form of the Verb

Use the command form of the verb for this paper. It is just like talking to someone.

After lighting the coals, **place** the bratwurst on the grill.

Turn left on 47th and Damen, and **head** west for three blocks.

The word "you" is understood with the command form of the verbs used in the examples above.

SPECIAL NOTE: All the ideas listed in Exercise 1 begin with the command form of the verb.

EXERCISE 2: Before filling out your think sheet, study the sample think sheet below. The resulting first draft follows.

Name _Don Flens_   Period __3__

HOW TO DO PAPER THINK SHEET

1. What is your subject? _Changing a flat tire_

2. What materials are needed? _spare tire, jack, wood, lug wrench, mallet_

3. List all the steps needed to complete your process. Be specific. NO ASSUMPTIONS!

STEPS	GLUE WORDS
A. locate the tire	
B. remove the tire, wood, wrench from trunk	
C. block the wheel	
D. pry the hubcap	
E. loosen the nuts counterclockwise	
F. raise the jack	
G.	ETC.

4. Tentative Controlling Ideas _Changing a flat tire is easy if you follow a step-by-step procedure._

HELPFUL HINT: After you list your ideas, read the steps aloud. Visualize what you have written. See if there are gaps.

SUPER SPECIAL HINT: If you cannot complete this think sheet, throw it away. Maybe you don't know enough about your subject. Start again!

How to Change a Flat Tire

1. Changing a flat tire is a task almost everyone must tackle at least once in a lifetime, so knowing how to do it properly will make the job easier. 2. After locating the flat tire, determine which end of the car should be raised. 3. Open the trunk and remove the spare tire, jack, block of wood, and lug wrench. 4. Block the wheel so the car doesn't roll when the jack is set up. 5. Using the flat blade on one end of the lug wrench, pry the hubcap off the flat tire, exposing the lug nuts. 6. Now, fit the socket end of the lug wrench over one of the nuts, and loosen it by turning it counterclockwise. 7. Do not remove the nuts until all of them have been loosened. 8. Now raise the car making sure the jack is securely set under the bumper. 9. Begin pumping the jack with firm, smooth, steady strokes until the tire is about six inches above the ground. 10. Then unscrew the rest of the nuts with your fingers. 11. Place all the nuts in the hubcap so they will not be misplaced. 12. After grasping the flat tire firmly, pull it off the lug bolts and roll it aside. 13. Now position the spare tire over the bolts, and using your fingers, screw the lug nuts. 14. Now tighten each lug nut with the wrench, using the same amount of force on each nut. 15. Be careful not to strip the bolts by tightening the nuts too tightly. 16. Before fitting the hubcap back onto the tire, lower the car slowly and gently to the ground. 17. Remove the jack, and pound the hubcap back onto the tire with a soft rubber mallet. 18. Take the jack, lug wrench, block of wood, and mallet, and put them back into the trunk. 19. The flat tire is now changed, but make certain you take the damaged tire to a gas station to have it repaired as soon as possible.

Answer the following questions about **How to Change a Flat Tire.**

1. What is the controlling idea?
2. Does the paper follow a step-by-step procedure?
3. Are there any missing steps? Are any steps out of order?
4. Should more steps be added to make the explanation clearer?
5. What glue words did the writer use?
6. How did the paper end? Was the concluding sentence effective?

Think Sheet

With your subject selected, it is time to collect your thoughts on a think sheet. A think sheet is a list of ideas that will go into your first draft. It enables you to check to see if you know enough about your subject.

If you find yourself having a difficult time jotting down ideas, maybe you should regroup and switch topics. That is okay. That is the purpose of this sheet.

If your think sheet covers too many areas, you might need to narrow your subject.

A think sheet serves as a useful tool for brainstorming and ordering ideas.

After you complete your think sheet, your teacher might want to duplicate a volunteer copy for class discussion purposes. In fact, you might want to exchange think sheets with a classmate.

Name _____ Period _____

HOW TO DO PAPER THINK SHEET

1. What is your subject? _____

2. What materials are needed? _____
_____

3. List all the steps needed to complete your process. Be specific. NO ASSUMPTIONS!!

      STEPS   GLUE WORDS

A. _____

B. _____

C. _____

D. _____

E. _____

F. _____

G. _____

H. _____

4. Tentative Controlling Idea _____
_____

HELPFUL HINT: After you list your ideas, read the steps aloud. Visualize what you have written. See if there are any gaps.

SUPER SPECIAL HINT: If you cannot complete this think sheet, throw it away. Maybe you don't know enough about your subject. Start again!!

STAGE TWO: WRITING THE FIRST DRAFT

Write your first draft with your think sheet in front of you. Be sure to number your sentences and skip every other line. This makes it easier for your partner to proofread your paper. The extra space also allows for corrections.

In writing your first draft, do not worry about mechanical errors. Make sure you have all the necessary ideas written down.

Here are some things to consider as you write your first draft:

1. The controlling idea should state the subject.
2. The paper should be organized in a step-by-step sequence.
3. Each step should be fully explained.
4. The ideas must follow a time sequence. Glue words should be used to glue ideas together.
5. The ending should be the last step. You might want to make some final comment on the finished product.
6. The verbs should be in the command form.

NOW WRITE YOUR FIRST DRAFT! Reread it carefully and circle the main verbs.

Sentence Opening Sheet

Once you have written your first draft, fill out a sentence opening sheet. The SOS "help" sheet will assist you in locating errors you need to correct before writing the first draft.

Here are the symbols to put above each column on the Sentence Opening Sheet.

Var, Frag First Four Words	Glue Special	Var, Tense Command Verbs	RO, Var # of words per sentence

As you study the Sentence Opening Sheet, ask yourself these questions about the columns:

Column One   **First Four Words**

1. Do all of my sentences begin with the command form of the verb?
2. Can I combine and/or rearrange some sentences to make them more interesting?
3. Do any of my sentences begin with glue words? Are these possibly sentence fragments?
4. Do I overuse "you" in my sentence openings?

Column Two   **Special**

1. Did I occasionally use a glue word to show the shift of ideas?

Column Three   **Verbs**

1. Are all my verbs in the command form?
2. Did I repeat the same verbs over and over again?
3. Could I make the paper more interesting by using specific, colorful, and active verbs?

Column Four   **Number of Words Per Sentence**

1. Are any of my overly long sentences run-ons?
2. Can I make my sentences more interesting by combining some of the shorter ones?

SPECIAL HINT: The purpose of the Sentence Opening Sheet is to help you spot items which may need to be corrected. You can make these corrections on the "skipped spaces" of your first draft.

Examine the sample Sentence Opening Sheet on the following page. It goes along with the sample paragraph, **How to Change a Flat Tire**.

NAME: Dan Flens   PERIOD: 3

How to Change a Flat Tire

VAR FRAG SENTENCE OPENING (First Four Words)	GLUE SPECIAL	VAR-COMMAND VERBS	VAR RO # OF WORDS PER SENTENCE
① Changing a flat tire		is	29
		must tackle	
② After locating the flat	after	determine	14
		should be raised	
③ Open the trunk and		open	15
		remove	
④ Block the wheel so		block	14
		doesn't roll	
⑤ Using the flat blade		pry	22
⑥ Now, fit the socket	now	fit	22
		loosen	
⑦ Do not remove the	until	do not remove	12
		have been loosened	
⑧ Now raise the car	now	raise	14
⑨ Begin pumping the jack	until	begin	19
		is	
	(ETC.)		

STAGE THREE: REWRITING

In the rewriting stage you should correct all the mistakes from the first draft, using the Sentence Opening Sheet and the feedback you receive from your partner or support group. Try to make your final draft error free. Before you submit your final draft, read it aloud or have someone else read it aloud to you. This helps you to hear mistakes that might otherwise go unnoticed.

EXERCISE 3: Before exchanging papers, criticize this student first draft as a group activity. Use your checklist sheet as your guide. Refer to the proofreading marks on page 158 to indicate mechanical errors.

SPECIAL NOTE: Instead of using this model, one or two volunteers might submit their first draft for discussion purposes.

Previewing a History Chapter

1. To improve your grade in history class, you should learn how to preview a unit before you begin reading it. 2. First, you should read the chapter's title and all subtitles. 3. You should stop and think about the key ideas that are mentioned in these chapter titles and subtitles. 4. Now you should go to the end of the chapter and read the summary paragraph. 5. Which gives you the main ideas covered in a condensed form. 6. Now you should look to see if the chapter has questions at the end normally these questions give you the specific ideas your teacher will be looking for. 7. Also, as you read the chapter you should look for the specific answers to these questions at the end of the chapter. 8. Now you should look for any pictures, graphs, or cartoons see if they have captions underneath them. 9. Skim the entire chapter and look for any repeated names or ideas.

SUPPLEMENTAL EXERCISE: These student sentences contain common errors found in "How to Do" compositions. They have been included as supplemental exercises if you need more work on spotting fragments, run-ons, and overuse of the word "you."

                      Frag
EXAMPLE: Although patching up a bicycle tire might seem difficult. It is easy if you follow these directions.

REWRITTEN: Although patching up a bicycle tire might seem difficult, it is easy if you follow these directions.

RO

EXAMPLE: Fill up the tire tube with air now put it in a bucket of water.

REWRITTEN: Fill up the tire tube with air. Now put it in a bucket of water.

1. Next, set your hands on the sides of the basketball bring the ball up to your chest. Leaving 10 to 12 inches between the ball and chest.
2. In washing clothes separating the colored materials from the white stuff.
3. When changing a baby's diaper, wear a mask over your face spray the mask with perfume.
4. Add a pinch of salt to a quart pot filled with water. Then boil the water add the spaghetti.
5. After you open the box of cake mix, you pour the ingredients into a large bowl you now add eggs and you add a ½ cup of milk.
6. Squeeze a small amount of toothpaste to the brush. Now brushing your front and back teeth using an up and down motion.
7. After the sheet is firmly tucked in. Pull up and smooth the bedspread again.
8. First, one should look up the country code in the telephone directory then one should look up the city code in the telephone directory.
9. After completely drying the car with old towels. Rub small amounts of wax in a circular motion in two foot areas.
10. First, read the essay question carefully. Looking for key terms like "discuss," "compare," and "explain."

Peer Evaluation Using a Checklist Sheet

Before writing your final draft, exchange papers with a proofreading partner. Your teacher might also put you in support groups.

Read your partner's paper two or three times so you understand the content. Then, using the questions from the checklist sheet, criticize the paper. Correct all the errors. Treat the paper as if it were your own.

Writer's Name _____

Corrector's Name _____

HOW TO DO CHECKLIST

1. Write out the controlling idea in the space provided. Mark the key words.

2. Does the controlling idea state the subject of the paper?

3. What is the subject?

4. Does the writer organize the ideas in a step-by-step sequence?

5. Number the steps on the first draft.

6. Are there any missing steps, gaps? If so, indicate where they are on the first draft.

7. Are there any ideas that do not contribute to the paper's purpose? If so, mark "subtract" above them on the first draft.

8. Are all the verbs in the command form? Mark any which are not in the correct form.

9. Circle all the glue words used to indicate a shift from one idea to the next. **HINT:** first, now, then, finally, etc.

10. Indicate if any sentences should be combined and/or rearranged to make more interesting sentences. **HINT:** variety in openings and lengths.

11. Does the writer use the word "you" too frequently in the paper?

12. How did the paper end? Does the writer end with the final step or make a comment on the process?

13. Mark all mechanical errors.

UNIT FIVE   PERSONAL NARRATIVE PAPER

Everyone has a story to tell. The purpose of this unit, then, is for you to tell a story from the first person point of view.

STAGE ONE: PREWRITING

Student Learning Objectives

1. The student will write a story about a personal experience using the first person personal pronouns.
2. The student will limit the time, space, action, and characters in the story.
3. The student will plunge immediately into the action of the story in the beginning of the paper or begin with a thematic opening.
4. The student will organize the story in a chronological sequence.
5. The student will supply specific supportive ideas so the audience shares in the writer's feelings.
6. The student will link the story's ideas by using first person pronouns and/or by using glue "time" words.
7. The student will keep all verbs in the past tense.
8. The student will conclude the story with a lasting impression of the events or with a clincher sentence.

Helpful Drills

Before you begin working on this assignment, practice some simple sentence combining techniques. In the **SENTENCE MANIPULATION** unit, you combined sentences in a variety of ways. Now you will concentrate on combining sentences using glue words (subordinating conjunctions) and WH words (relative pronouns). This will help you in two ways. First, you will learn how to stress main ideas in your sentences by subordinating lesser ideas. Second, you will learn how to identify and correct sentence fragments.

An idea that is important should be in a sentence by itself. Glue words and WH words introduce lesser or subordinate ideas. Consequently, groups of words introduced by glue words and WH words are fragments. Here are some examples:

GLUE WORD FRAGMENT: Because Jenny loves MTV.
WH WORD FRAGMENT: Which caused Lamont to yell.

The following two sentences are both complete ideas.

Frankie Dirmush broke the window.
Frankie was punished.

You may want to combine these two sentences into one. However, before you do this, decide which of the two ideas is more important. If the more important idea is "Frankie Dirmush was punished," you might write:

A. Frankie Dirmush was punished **because he broke the window.**

Notice that "Frankie Dirmush was punished" could stand by itself. "Because he broke the window" is a fragment. The main verb in this sentence is "was punished" and would be the verb written on the Sentence Opening Sheet.

However, if you wanted to stress "Frankie broke the window," you might combine the original pair in this way:

B. Frankie Dirmush broke the window **because he was punished.**

In this sentence "broke" is the main verb.

For both these sentences, the sentence part with greatest impact is the one **not** introduced by the glue word (subordinating conjunction) "because." The main verb changes with the location of the main idea of the sentence. Also, note how the meaning changes between these two sentences.

Glue Words

Here is a list of glue words (subordinating conjunctions):

TIME: as, after, before, since, until, when, whenever, while
CAUSE OR REASON: because, since
CONDITION: if, although, as long as, though, unless, even if, even though, as if
PURPOSE: so that, in order that
PLACE: where, wherever

EXERCISE 1: Combine the following sentences using the glue words listed above. First determine which idea is more important. You want to create IMPACT. Then add the glue word before the lesser idea. Try more than one glue word with each pair.

SPECIAL PUNCTUATION RULE: When a sentence begins with a glue word (subordinating conjunction), put a comma after the first clause. When the glue word is mid-sentence, there is no comma.

EXAMPLE: Steve cleans his bedroom.
His mother smiles in delight.

REWRITTEN: A. **Whenever Steve cleans his bedroom**, his mother **smiles in delight.**
REWRITTEN: B. His mother smiles in delight **whenever Steve cleans his room.**

Notice the second example has no comma because the glue word is in the middle of the sentence.

1. The volleyball referee called Hilda for hitting the net. The coach screamed in protest.
2. The lights went out. The fuse blew.
3. Spencer Spud flunked geography and science. He will be promoted to the ninth grade.
4. Vinnie Fifano stays on his diet three months. He will lose forty pounds.
5. The train was coming into the depot. Sylvester was running down the ramp.
6. Izzy Pool can swim. He must take a shower in the locker room area.
7. His phone will be disconnected. Willie Wilcox pays the bill.
8. Her hands hurt. The gymnast just finished her third routine.
9. Harriet cannot shoot free throws. She practices daily in the gym.
10. Spizzy Pfants cannot go to the washroom. The lunch bell rings.
11. There will be trouble. Jonni Comelate sits in the back of the room.
12. The tomatoes started to grow. They were planted in the fertilized soil.
13. The tornado struck the downtown area. The National Guard patrolled the streets.
14. The teachers lost two weeks pay. They lined up in front of the unemployment office.
15. Herb Haub received a knuckle sandwich. He smashed Serena with a 2 x 4.

Glue Word Fragments

An incomplete thought is called a sentence fragment. It is only part or a fragment of a sentence.

Glue words (subordinating conjunctions) show how two clauses are related. However, if the clause that begins with the glue word is left by itself without the main idea, a fragment results.

Often students write glue word fragments because their minds work faster than they are able to write. They start a second idea before finishing the first, or they omit a key word.

Also, in their haste to reread their sentences, they combine ideas that are written as separate word groups. Read the following. See if you can identify the fragment.

As the waves pounded the boat. Kevin desperately tried to start the motor.

Which group of words in the above example is a fragment?

EXERCISE 2: The following word groups are glue word fragments. Correct each sentence by expanding with your own ideas. Punctuate your expanded sentences correctly. (**NOTE:** Work for variety by not always locating the glue word at the beginning of the sentence.)

EXAMPLE: Because Rover chewed up Amy's boot.

REWRITTEN: Because Rover chewed up Amy's boot, Amy's father locked him in the cellar.

or

We laughed **because** Rover chewed up Amy's boot.

1. Even though Santa Claus slid down the chimney.
2. Unless the doctor signs the excuse.
3. While Cynthia played the first trombone in the concert band.
4. Because everyone would be invited.
5. After John Hickey lit the stick of dynamite.
6. Until Jamie quits talking.
7. Since the water overflowed the sink.
8. Although the Seattle Seahawks defeated the Los Angeles Raiders.
9. Whenever the lights go out.
10. Before Scott watered the lawn.

WH Words

Another way of combining sentences is to use WH words (relative pronouns). These WH words replace a repeated person, activity, or thing. They are placed next to the word or words they replace. Here is a list of WH words:

WHO	people
WHOSE	people (possession)
WHOM	people
WHICH	things and actions
*THAT	things and actions

*THAT doesn't begin with WH, but it is still a WH word because it does the same job as the other WH words in a sentence.

Here are some examples of sentences combined with WH words.

EXAMPLES: The cab driver parked in front of the fire plug.
The cab driver received a parking ticket.

REWRITTEN: A. The cab driver **who parked in front of the fire plug** received a parking ticket.

The main idea is "The cab driver received a parking ticket." However, if you want to stress the idea "The cab driver parked in front of the fire plug," you might write this:

REWRITTEN: B. The cab driver **who received a parking ticket** parked in front of the fire plug.

Here is another example:

Water skiing is a summer activity.
Water skiing sometimes causes injuries.

Water skiing, **which is a summer activity,** sometimes causes injuries.

Which is the main idea in the above sentence? How do you know?

SPECIAL PUNCTUATION RULE: If the WH clause is necessary or important to the meaning of the sentence, do not add commas.

However, if the WH clause contains extra information not necessary or important to the sentence's meaning, add commas before and after the clause.

Here are two examples. Explain why example A has commas and example B does not.

A. The fire started in the cellar.
   The fire sent up great clouds of smoke.

   The fire, **which started in the cellar**, sent up great clouds of smoke.

B. The man who won the lottery.
   The man sat behind me.

   The man **who won the lottery** sat behind me.

EXERCISE 3: Combine the following sentences using WH words (relative pronouns). First determine which group of words is the more important idea. Then place the appropriate WH word before the second idea. After you combine each pair once, try combining a second time, changing the main idea. Punctuate correctly.

1. Joey Sludge cleans sewers. Joey makes a superb quiche.
2. Sid Slique models men's clothing. He is tall, dark, and ugly.
3. Maxie tries cases in the Federal Building. She is married to Judge Menot.
4. Smackerover, Florida, won the national championship of the "Anything Goes" TV show. The town received eight tons of caviar.
5. Winthrop's wife presented him with triplets. He spends his spare hours washing diapers.
6. Larry cannot swim. He is the lifeguard at the Palos Pool.
7. Roak's Diner serves excellent barbeque ribs. It has polka music on the weekends.
8. Barb Bend holds a doctor's degree in history. She waits on tables for a part time job.
9. Ned Storm forecasts the weather. He predicted the thunderstorms for this evening.
10. Roxanne spent six days in the hospital. She was in an accident on Carp Stew Festival Day.

WH Word Fragments

Like glue words, WH word clauses cannot stand alone as a

sentence. Unfortunately, some writers mistakenly place periods after WH clauses, treating them as sentences. Here are examples:

Which belongs to Stacey.

>or

The squirrel **which** scooted down the tree.

One way to correct these WH word fragments is to expand.

The Cabbage Patch doll which belongs to Stacey **is bald.**.

The squirrel which scooted down the tree **gathered up a pile of nuts**.

EXERCISE 4: Expand each WH word fragment, making it a complete thought. Punctuate your WH clauses correctly.

1. The leaning tower of Pisa **which was straightened out.**
2. The sausage factory **which imports Polish hams.**
3. The little boy **who answered the girl's call for help.**
4. The paddy wagon **which contained the mob of rioters.**
5. **That fell off the bench.**
6. The girl **who cuts the lawn for her neighbors.**
7. **Which had been left by Mrs. Winebald years before.**
8. Mr. Peabody **whose cat was bitten by the bird.**
9. The busboy to **whom you spoke.**
10. **Who sings in the choir.** (Note: not a question)

Subject

The purpose of this paper is for you to narrate a story about some incident that happened to you. Your incident can be an ordinary experience. For example, you might write about your anxiety and nervousness in giving your first speech. Or you might write about your embarrassment and/or fright in getting caught doing something you shouldn't have been doing. Maybe you were a hero or a "goat" in the final seconds of a basketball or volleyball game, etc.

The incident you select must be limited in time, space, characters, and action. In other words, you are better off fully describing some small, significant incident instead of writing about an entire day's trip to Disneyland, etc. You are expected to tell not only what happened, but how you felt during the incident.

The choice of the subject is yours. Select a memorable incident that has meaning for you. Here are some suggested ideas to get you thinking:

1. What was the most embarrassing moment in your life? What happened first? Second? How did you feel at the beginning, middle, end? What were the surroundings like?
2. What was the most frightening incident you ever experienced? What happened? How did you feel?
3. What was the most heroic deed you ever performed?
4. What was the most frustrating event that ever happened to you?
5. What incident in your life caused you the most exhilaration? The most joy?
6. What was the funniest incident you have ever been involved in?

As a group activity, you might want to discuss some of the ideas from the previous list. Share some of your experiences. Visualize.

Here are more suggested topics:

1. Getting caught coming home after curfew.
2. Opening a special birthday gift.
3. Witnessing a crime, accident, etc.
4. Describing an exciting moment in a sporting event.
5. Asking that "special someone" for a date.
6. What about some incidents that happened at home, school, forest preserves, etc.?
7. What about the great success or greatest failure you have ever experienced?

As a group activity, brainstrom. Talk about some possible topics.

Controlling Idea

You have two choices for beginning your composition. First, you can plunge immediately into your story's action. The first sentence of "The Frightening Walk" example on page 65 uses this type of beginning. Second, since incidents often illustrate a theme or general idea, your first sentence might be a controlling idea which gives an overview. Here is an example:

SAMPLE CONTROLLING IDEA: Nothing is more valuable to me than a good friend. On Christmas Eve in 1983, I decided to trick my dad . . .

Whatever type of beginning you decide to use, remember that you want to arouse your reader's interest. Make your reader want to read on.

Organizing the Paper

After you have selected your incident, jot down all the ideas about it you can remember. As a thinking exercise, ask yourself these questions:

1. What actions did I perform in this incident?
2. What happened at the beginning? How did I feel? Did the setting affect my feelings?
3. What happened with each action? How did I feel?
4. What were the surroundings like?
5. Did I feel different at the end than I did at the beginning?

Think of all the little details that happened in the beginning, middle, and ending sequences. Try to visualize what happened.

You should organize your ideas in the actual sequence in which they occurred. Expand each action with specific details. This will make your story more interesting for your reader. It is not enough that you recount the events. Your reader should share in your feelings.

Gluing Together Ideas

Since this paper will follow a time sequence, you can use glue words that indicate time. Here is a brief list:

GLUE WORDS (transitions): once, then, now, soon, while, finally, suddenly, after a few seconds

Think of others!

Another way of linking ideas is by using repeated pronouns. This links the ideas. Read the following excerpt from a student composition. Note the use of pronouns and time glue words.

Sudden Fright

1. Until the moment **I** began **my** speech, **I** had not felt at all nervous. 2. Walking proudly to the podium, **I** noticed a deep feeling of confidence swelling up inside of **me**. 3. Coughs, grumbles, and whispers echoed

throughout the auditorium as **I** put **my** notes in place. 4. Suddenly butterflies formed within **my** stomach as the words wouldn't come out of **my** mouth. 5. The once steady heart beat increased twofold as sweat moistened **my** hands. 6. Then . . .

Here is a list of first person pronouns:

PRONOUNS   I   we
        my, mine   our, ours
          me   us

Ending

You should plan your ending just as you plan your beginning. For this paper you may choose from two different types of endings. The final action in your incident may leave a lasting impression, so you need not write another sentence. On the other hand, you may end with a short statement or comment on the meaning of this incident. Whichever you choose, make sure the ending leaves the reader with the feeling your incident is over. The verb tense may change in this final clinching sentence. As a final step, give the paper a title that captures the meaning or mood of your incident and makes the reader just a little curious about the incident you are about to relate.

EXERCISE 5: Before you begin to fill out your think sheet, study the sample student compositions. Use these questions as a guide for class discussion purposes.

1. What is the incident described?
2. How is it limited in time, space, character, and action?
3. What type of beginning did the writer use? Does the writer begin with a thematic controlling idea, or did the writer plunge immediately into the story's action?
4. Are the events written in time sequence?
5. Does the writer supply specific feelings with the story's actions?
6. How did the writer glue together ideas? Are glue words and/or repeated pronouns used?
7. Are all the verbs in the past tense?
8. What type of ending did the writer use?

A Frightening Walk

1. One single thought, getting home early, raced through my mind as I shivered in the crisp autumn air. 2. Hoping to save an extra mile, I decided to take a short cut through the cemetery. 3. Cautiously I entered the large, metal gates. 4. While I walked past an old white marble mausoleum, a scary feeling overcame me as dark, billowy clouds blotted out the peacefully setting orange sun. 5. A dog painfully howled in the distance. 6. Gusting winds made the large, haunting black trees sway violently. 7. My imagination took control 8. I visioned crows as ravens and sparrows as hawks. 9. Birds flocked on the bare trees which formed frightening figures against the blackening sky. 10. An owl perched on a tombstone sent a chill up and down my spine as my body quivered with fright. 11. I began running past swaying oak trees and down the narrow, gravel path. 12. The pavement had become considerably narrower and almost impassable as I ran between the rows of tombstones. 13. A surge of joy filled me as I could see the iron gates ten yards ahead. 14. I knew I was nearly home. 15. Walking on a carpet of green wet grass, I calmly passed through the large iron gates.

Late at Night

1. One dark, cold night while carefreely walking home from Marquette Park, I noticed a suspicious looking car following me. 2. Cold chills ran up and down my spine as I recalled a similar experience. 3. My heart pounded two forty as the car pulled up behind me and stopped. 4. Through the dim light I could see three boys staring at me. 5. I walked faster. 6. Out of the corner of my eye, I saw two of them get out of the car. 7. Terrified, I ran as I had never run before. 8. Seeing a group of young kids standing on the corner, I breathlessly approached them. 9. At that moment I became hysterical. 10. I shook violently and was unable to tell them what was happening. 11. Finally, I regained my composure and explained the circumstances. 12. They offered to accompany me home to make sure I arrived there safely. 13. After walking about half a block, I noticed the car again. 14. It stopped and parked behind us. 15. I was petrified. 16. I clung tightly to the arm of one of the boys who was walking me home. 17. Again I became hysterical and began to cry. 18. The boys accompanying me calmed me down as we approached my house. 19. Thanking them, I ran up the porch to safety. 20. This experience remains with me every time I walk home late at night.

NOTE: The verb in sentence 19 "remains" changed to present tense. This change in tense is permissible for the concluding sentence which makes a comment on the experience.

Think Sheet

By now you probably have selected a topic for this personal narrative composition. Before you begin to write your first draft, however, explore your topic to see if you have enough information. That is the purpose of this think sheet. In a concrete way this think sheet helps you to review the events of your special incident.

Remember, your audience does not know anything about your incident. Your job is to make the story interesting by recounting the events and sharing your feelings. Colorful adjectives, adverbs, and verbs will aid you in creating a realistic incident in which your audience can share.

Name _____ Period _____

PERSONAL NARRATIVE THINK SHEET

1. What type of story are you going to tell? _____
   _____

2. How much time was covered? _____

3. Where did the incident take place? _____

4. Who were the participants besides yourself? _____
   _____

5. Jot down the events in the actual sequence in which they occurred. Also, list the specific ideas that happened with each event. Here are some questions to help you think through the events and the specific details.

   What specific actions happened in this event? How did you feel with each action? What physical signs indicated your feeling, i.e. sweaty palms, shaky knees? What were the surroundings like with each happening? What were some of your thoughts with each happening? Expand using the journalistic questions. (who, what, when, where, why, how)

   The Happenings   **Specific Details**

   1. The beginning: _____

   2. _____

   3. _____

   4. _____

   5. _____

   6. _____

   7. The ending: _____

SPECIAL HINT: With each event, expand with specific details.

Rules for Writing Dialogue

Although you do not have to use dialogue in this paper, we have included some rules for writing dialogue in case you decide to use it. Here are some standard punctuation rules for dialogue writing.

1. Begin a direct quotation with a capital letter.

    Tommy yelled, "**Pass** the dumplings."

2. Use quotation marks to enclose a direct quotation.

    Jennifer screamed, "I want a Cabbage Patch doll for my birthday."

3. A direct quotation is set off from the rest of the sentence by commas.

    "You shouldn't have eaten the chocolate cake," said Aunt Myrna, "without my permission."

4. When a quoted sentence is divided in two parts by expressions such as "he said," "she replied," "Jack mentioned," the second part begins with a small letter.

    "I know, " muttered Aggie, "**that** you are wrong."

5. If the second part of the broken quotation is a new sentence, it begins with a capital letter.

    "The movie just started," said the usher. "**You** will still be able to see all of it."

6. When you write dialogue, begin a new paragraph every time the speaker changes.

    "Hello, Wendy," said Robin softly. "What should we buy Uncle Wally for his birthday?"

    "Nothing," yelled Wendy. "He has everything already!"

7. If a quotation is only a fragment of a sentence, do not begin it with a capital letter.

    Vinnie denied that he was a "**yellow** chicken liver" because he would not walk into the haunted house.

8. Do not use quotation marks to enclose an indirect quotation—not the speaker's exact words. The key word "that" tells us these are not the speaker's exact words.

   Jennifer said **that** she wanted a Cabbage Patch doll for her birthday.

9. Other marks of punctuation when used with quotation marks are placed according to the following rules:

   A. Commas and periods are always placed **inside** the closing quotation mark.

      "I don't know the answer," answered Stacey, "but I know where to get it."

   B. Colons and semicolons are always placed **outside** the closing quotation marks.

      Mr. Zigmond said to us: "You all made the team"; what he said after that I don't remember.

      The following volleyball players have, in the words of the **Portland Oregonian**, "surpassed all expectations": Valerie Maguire, Hal Hedson, and Jeremy Brick.

   C. Question marks and exclamation points are placed **inside** the closing quotation marks if the quotation is a question or an exclamation; otherwise, they are placed **outside**.

      "Are the players ready?" asked the umpire.
      "How angry you are sometimes!" Mollie muffled.

      Were you angry when he said, "Drop dead"?

      How said it was to hear her say, "You failed English"!

10. When a quoted passage consists of more than one paragraph, place the quotation marks at the **beginning of each paragraph** and at the **end of the entire passage**, not at the end of each paragraph.

STAGE TWO: WRITING THE FIRST DRAFT

With your completed think sheet in front of you, write the first draft. Don't forget to skip every other line and number sentences.

Do not be concerned with mechanical errors. Just get the words on paper. Here is a review of some things to consider as you write:

1. Begin by plunging into the action of the narrative, or writing a general statement (CI) which captures the theme.
2. Organize your ideas with a beginning, middle, and an ending.
3. Supply specific feelings with each of the actions. Let the reader experience what you felt.
4. Use glue words (time) and/or repeat pronouns to link ideas.
5. Keep verbs in **past** tense.
6. End in an interesting fashion.

NOW WRITE YOUR FIRST DRAFT! Reread it carefully and circle each main verb.

Sentence Opening Sheet

After the first draft is completed, reread the draft, circle the main verbs, and fill out the four columns of the Sentence Opening Sheet. Here are some symbols to put above each column:

Frag, Var	PN	Var, VP, Tense	Var, RO
First Four Words	Special	Verbs	Number of words per sentence

Now that your first draft is completed and the Sentence Opening Sheet is filled out, check each column for the following:

Column One   **First Four Words**

1. Do all of my sentences begin with the same openings, especially the word "I?"

2. Can any of my sentences be combined and/or rearranged to make them more interesting?
3. Do any of my sentences begin with a glue word or ING words making them perhaps a fragment?

Column Two   **Special**

1. Did I shift from first person pronoun by using "you?"

Column Three   **Verbs**

1. Are all my verbs in the past tense?
2. Do I repeat the same weak verbs over and over again, especially "was," "were," "got," or "had?"
3. Could I make any of my sentences more interesting by using concrete verbs?

Column Four   **Number of Words Per Sentence**

1. Do any of my sentences contain too many words? Are these overly long sentences run-ons?
2. Can I make some of my sentences more interesting by combining the short choppy ones? **NOTE:** In this paper, some short sentences create **IMPACT** by the emotion contained.

STAGE THREE: REWRITING

Before you rewrite your final draft, you will need to exchange papers with a proofreading partner or work in a support group. However, first see if you can spot any errors in this student first draft.

EXERCISE 6: Criticize this student first draft. Use your checklist sheet or questions from Exercise 5 as your guide. Refer to the proofreading marks on page 158 to note mechanical errors.

The Recital

1. I have never been more nervous as when I gave my first piano recital. 2. I sat in a huge auditorium, and I wait for my name to be called. 3. I tapped my fingers on my knees. 4. I feel the sweat pour from my forehead. 5. Being very nervous, I got up

and went backstage to practice my piece. 6. I was too fidgety. 7. I decided to forget the whole thing and try to sneak out the backdoor. 8. Then I heard my name being called, "Jamie Hanlon." 9. Now I couldn't leave. 10. I knew I have three minutes before my turn would begin. 11. My heart pounded as I walked up to the main stage. 12. I look at the keyboard, and I couldn't remember the song that I was suppose to play. 13. Suddenly all became still. 14. I wanted to cry. 15. As I began to touch down on the keys. 16. I prayed time would go quickly. 17. Everything came back to me, and I got control of myself. 18. I felt more and more confident as I progressed into the song. 19. The butterflies were gone, and I felt in complete control. 20. As the song ended, I felt relieved. 21. Slowly I stood up and practically ran back to my place. 22. The ovation I received made the whole nerve wracking experience worthwhile.

SUPPLEMENTAL EXERCISE: These student sentences contain fragment and run-on errors. First, identify the error, and second, rewrite the corrected sentence on a separate sheet of paper.

1. I dropped the ice cream. Which quickly melted in the boiling sun.
2. As my palms sweated and my knees rattled. I threw the ticking package into the toilet bowl.
3. I ran through the cemetery gate I dodged behind the Toyota van I peeked around the corner.
4. The truck driver stepped out of his truck and waved his hand angrily at me. Just because I hit his window with a snowball.
5. The second time I approached the line I dropped the bowling ball on my toe. Which caused me to scream hysterically.
6. I bounced the ball three, four, five times. While a hush came over the crowd.
7. If I didn't complete the jump. Everyone could consider me a big chicken.
8. Slyly I took the notes from my pocket I hid them under the paper the exam began.
9. As I heard my name being called. I hesitated for a moment then walked out onto the stage.
10. Gingerly I walked up to Mr. Barbosa. The teacher whom everyone feared.

Peer Evaluation Using a Checklist Sheet

Now exchange papers with a proofreading partner, or your teacher might put you in support groups.

So you understand the content of your partner's paper, read the paper two or three times before you begin to criticize it. Use the questions from the checklist sheet as your guide. Treat this paper as if it were your own.

Writer's Name _____

Corrector's Name _____

PERSONAL NARRATIVE CHECKLIST

1. Write the controlling idea in the space provided.
2. Was the opening interesting? Why or why not?
3. What is the story about?
4. What is the time span for the incident?
5. Where does the story take place?
6. Are the events written in time sequence? Mark any event out of sequence on the first draft.
7. Are there any gaps? That is, are there any places where the writer needs to expand? Mark them on the first draft.
8. Does the writer supply specific feelings? Mark the most vivid.
9. Circle the glue words and/or repeat pronoun used to link ideas.
10. Does the writer keep all the verbs in the past tense? Note any which are not in past tense.
11. Does the writer vary sentence openings? Mark the need for variety on the first draft.
12. What type of ending did the writer use? Was it effective?
13. Mark any glue words or WH word fragments.
14. Mark any run-ons.
15. Mark any other mechanical errors you find.

UNIT SIX SPATIAL DEVELOPMENT PAPER

A good writer should be able to describe a room so the reader sees it. For this paper, you'll describe a ransacked kitchen.

STAGE ONE: PREWRITING

Student Learning Objectives

1. The student will describe a room, organizing the ideas in a spatial development order, i.e., right to left, left to right, foreground to background, etc.
2. The student will use past participles to describe objects in the room.
3. The student will learn the different functions of present participles, ING words.
4. The student will keep all verbs in the present tense.
5. The student will link ideas using appropriate glue words.

Helpful Drills

In the **Personal Narrative** unit, you used ED words to describe past tense. Now you will learn to use part participles as adjectives. Note, however, that not all ED words end in ED, i.e., caug**ht**, froz**en**, pai**d**, thro**wn**.

Study the following examples to see ED words used as both verbs and adjectives.

EXAMPLES:

1. The boy **toppled** the table. — past tense verb
2. The table **toppled by the boy** rolled on the floor. — adjective-past-participle

3. The cat **spilled** the milk. — past tense verb
4. The milk **spilled by the cat** dripped down the cabinet. — adjective-past-participle

5. The ball **was thrown** by Ginger. — past tense verb
6. The ball **thrown by Ginger** broke Mrs. Humpdecker's window. — adjective-past-participle

We use past participles in our everyday conversation to describe people and objects. Here are a few examples:

written message	a door **closed by the wind**
a **broken** toe	a sink **filled with dirty dishes**
a **frightened** child	a thief **caught in the act**
a **wrecked** car	an old building **ravaged by fire**
burnt toast	my notes **stapled together**
a **fallen** tree	a desk **cluttered by school books**
split juice	an old man **forgotten by his family**
an **exhausted** mother	a mirror **smudged with fingerprints**

Can you think of more ED words used to describe? As a class, make a list.

SPECIAL HINT: Using a grammar book, look up a list of regular and irregular verbs. Use the past participles as adjectives.

EXERCISE 1: Expand the following ED words by adding details from your ransacked kitchen whenever possible. The examples already filled in may be changed to apply to your room. Be imaginative.

EXAMPLES: shoed
finger-smudged

REWRITTEN: **shoed** potato chips sitting on the floor
a **finger-smudged** refrigerator door

1. toppled _____
2. soiled _____
3. smudged _____
4. strewn (candy wrappers **strewn** about the table)
5. shattered _____
6. overturned _____
7. torn (**torn** magazine covers cluttering the counter)
8. spilled (split) _____
9. stained _____
10. honey smeared _____
11. ruffled _____
12. clogged _____
13. splattered _____
14. covered _____
15. cluttered _____
16. melted _____
17. puddled _____
18. crumpled (**crumpled** potato chip bags)
19. unwrapped _____
20. scattered _____
21. stacked _____
22. coated _____
23. caked (food **caked** over the door)
24. ransacked _____
25. dusted _____
26. swept _____

Subtracting Empty Words

In the **Sentence Manipulation** unit, you practiced subtracting repeated or unnecessary words. This revision skill is important in descriptive writing when you are trying to be concise.

EXERCISE 2: First, subtract the "empty" words by rearranging sentence parts. Second, expand when necessary. Try to write ED word clusters to describe specific objects. Keep verbs in the present tense, and write complete sentences — not fragments.

SPECIAL NOTE: Some of your sentences might be put on transparencies for discussion purposes. This exercise might be completed in small groups rather than individually.

EXAMPLE: The hot dog **which is** plump **which was** striped **which is** grilled and **which was** smeared with mustard.

REWRITTEN: The plump, grill-line striped, mustard-smeared hot dog (GOOD WORD CLUSTER—THIS NEEDS TO BE EXPANDED TO ELIMINATE THE FRAGMENT).

or

The grill-lined, mustard-smeared, plump hot dog (GOOD WORD CLUSTER—THIS NEEDS TO BE EXPANDED TO ELIMINATE THE FRAGMENT).

or

The grill-lined, mustard-smeared hot dog plumps. (PLUMPS BECOMES THE PRESENT-TENSE VERB COMPLETING THE PHRASE).

1. The pickle WHICH IS juicy WHICH IS pockmarked WHICH IS sour and WHICH IS green.
2. The gravy WHICH IS dripping from the platter WHICH IS smudged with fingers.
3. There IS a table WHICH IS made of mahogany WHICH IS shaded.
4. There IS a head of a moose WHICH IS stuffed WHICH IS hanging over the fireplace.
5. The sofa WHICH IS soaked with Pepsi and WHICH IS smeared with mustard and WHICH IS squished with chocolate syrup.

6. There IS a case WHICH IS made for guns and WHICH IS large and WHICH IS sturdy and WHICH IS made of pine wood.
7. There IS a chair WHICH IS vinyl and WHICH IS for reclining and WHICH IS dotted with spots WHICH ARE from milk.
8. There IS a sheet of glass WHICH IS broken and WHICH IS glistening.
9. There IS a rug WHICH IS a shag and WHICH IS green and WHICH IS lying in the center of the room.
10. There IS a burner WHICH IS for incense WHICH IS smoldering WHICH IS overturned.

After finishing this drill, go back to your samples of the first exercise. Could you make any of them more specific or colorful?

ING WORDS - Dangling and Misplaced Modifiers

In this paper you will describe a kitchen without any people in it. You will be writing from the eye of the camera. Since you probably will be using ING words, present participles, here are three uses of these words:

1. POSITION ING WORDS - Used to Indicate Location

    A. The **hanging** light fixture sags under the weight of the baseball caps.
       NOTE: "Hanging" also describes the light fixture.
    B. The crumpled wrappers **resting** in the corner reveal the chaotic condition of this room.

2. DESCRIPTIVE ING WORDS - Used to Describe

    A. The **glistening** windows...
    B. The **sliding** glass door...

3. ACTION ING WORDS - Used to show motion

    A. **Walking into the room,** Sally noticed the counter top filled with wrappers, bottletops, and empty pop cans.
    B. **Lying on the kitchen table**, the milk carton stood open.
       NOTE: The comma is placed after the ING phrase.

ING action words must be used carefully in this paper because "dangling modifiers" might result. Since no people are to be included in the paper, it would be possible to write sentences like those which follow:

- A. **Walking through the door**, a finger-smudged refrigerator shows signs of wear.

- B. **Going along the east wall**, polka dots of soda spray glisten on the butcher block counter.

In "A" it appears as if the finger-smudged refrigerator is walking. What about "B"?

EXERCISE 3: When writing ING action words in papers, be careful they are not "dangling" or misplaced. If they are "dangling," rearrange and expand to correct the error. Correct the errors from from the following sentences on a separate sheet of paper.

EXAMPLE: Looking into the kitchen, a white Kelvinator refrigerator occupies the northeast corner of the room.

Who is looking in to kitchen? The refrigerator?

REWRITTEN: A white Kelvinator refrigerator occupies the northeast corner of the kitchen.

1. Reading quietly, the words in the story seemed to come to life for Jay Bruno.
2. Driving leisurely through the countryside, many horses and cows were seen by the Budz family.
3. Riding his bike across the outfield, a baseball hit Grover in the head.
4. Scrounging for food in the garbage can, LaVerne found her little French Poodle full of bugs.
5. Filled with rocks and weeds, Mr. Clutcher raked the garden.
6. Trying for a triple, the outfielder threw out Eric Walters as he slid into third base.
7. Sizzling under the hot sun, the wave finally cooled off the lifeguard.
8. Frying in the pan, Mary Jane flipped over the bacon.
9. Sitting on the roof, a strange light appeared in the sky.
10. After landing in Scranton, the two-hour wait caused Myles to become angry.

11. Filled with layers of bologna, Julian packed the sandwiches into the picnic basket.
12. Screaming with pain, lightning caused the old oak to fall on Patricia.
13. Nibbling the grass by the roadside, old MacDonald found his lost goat.
14. Filled with curiosity, the Christmas stocking made little Laura excited.
15. Walking slowly down the alley, the motorcycle hit the old man.
16. Moving to the left, a counter sits with broken potato chips and smudged sardine and jelly sandwiches.
17. Starting in the southeast corner of the kitchen, a dishwasher sits covered with papers and pencils.
18. Looking in the kitchen, overturned milk cartons make milk drip off the counter.
19. Now moving onto the south wall, eggs are splattered next to the sink.
20. Going toward the north wall, a dog bed is ripped to pieces.

Subject

This is a subject you should enjoy writing about because you probably have had many experiences with such a room. The purpose of this paper is to describe the kitchen after it has been invaded by you and your friends.

The kitchen has been left spotless. After winning a volleyball or basketball game, you invite your teammates to help themselves to whatever food and drink they can find in the pantry, refrigerator, cabinets, etc. After an hour of "wolfing down" food, everyone leaves without bothering to clean up.

Describe the kitchen, including all the specific details that make this room a mess. Write this paper for an imaginary camera viewpoint, making NO personal references.

Alternate Topics

If the above topic does not suit your fancy, select one of the alternate topics below with teacher's approval, of course.

1. Describe a neat, thoroughly cleaned kitchen.
2. Describe your fantasy room. Your parents have won the lottery and have given you unlimited funds to decorate and furnish your room as you please.

3. Select a picture of a beautiful room from a popular magazine. Describe that room.
4. Describe your school corridor at the end of the year after the lockers have been cleaned out.
5. Describe the school cafeteria after your last lunch period and before it has been cleaned up.
6. Describe the gym after a dance or basketball game.
7. Describe your favorite room.

SPECIAL HINT: Rectangular rooms are easier to describe.

Controlling Idea

You do not need to supply some background information before you start to describe your selected room. Rather, your beginning should name an object which will serve as a starting point for your description. In this way all other objects can be located in reference to it.

SAMPLE CONTROLLING IDEA: At the center of the east wall sits an Amana refrigerator, slightly ajar and splattered with catsup and mustard.

In the above example the writer used the refrigerator as the starting point and placed it in the center of the east wall. Here is an example of a controlling idea that does not contain a starting point. It would cause problems for the reader trying to locate the objects in this room.

WEAK CONTROLLING IDEA: To the right of the door stands a Hotpoint microwave oven perched on top of a metal stand.

What is the difference between the two sample controlling ideas? Which one could you use to begin drawing a map of the room? Why?

Organizing the Paper

The room's description must be organized from left to right, right to left, etc. In other words, it must be organized in some logical order, so your reader can pinpoint each object.

Before you write your first draft, draw a rough sketch, a think sheet, placing items in their proper place. Draw this map while you are sitting in the room, if possible. If you have selected an alternate topic, your map think sheet should be your first order of business. Visualize the objects and place them in the proper location.

Also, describe each object fully. Be specific enough so any reader would be able to describe everything in your selected room.

Gluing Together Ideas

In this paper you must use glue words that show places. These glue words will point out where the different objects are located. Here is a list of glue words that show place:

GLUE WORDS: underneath, above, between, below, here, farther, across, there, beyond, nearby, upon, opposite to, on top of, on the opposite, left, right, behind, next to, along, directly opposite, northeast, southwest

Can you think of other words to locate objects in your room?

Verb Power

Be careful you do not use ED words as verbs in this paper. All main verbs must be written in present tense. Here is brief list of verbs you might use:

POSSIBLE VERBS: rests, lies, lays, sits, stands, contains, surrounds, covers, hangs, situates, positions, scatters, surrounds, separates, occupies, leans, engulfs, protrudes, overlaps, piles, bulges, overhangs, stretches, shines, flanks, faces, displays, emits, hides, etc.

All the above verbs are third person singular or -s form. To form the verb which agrees with a plural subject, simply drop the final "s" to form the infinitive or base form.

EXAMPLE:

Third Person Singular Verb

The table **sits** in the northeast corner cluttered with junk.

Infinitive (used with plural subject)

Books **lean** against the typewriter stand.

Taboo Words (Teacher Option)

Since this paper will be written from the camera viewpoint, there are certain pronouns which should not be used in the final draft—teacher option, of course.

Here they are:

First Person Pronouns: I, we, us, my, mine, our, ours
Second Person Pronouns: you, your

Also, here are some verbs considered taboo:

TABOO VERBS: was, were   Why? They are past tense.

EXERCISE 4: Rewrite the following sentences to eliminate the taboo words. (**HINT:** Use no personal pronouns; use vivid verbs and expand.)

EXAMPLE: Our footprints were muddy.

REWRITTEN: Muddy footprints mark the path across the room.

1. Our fingerprints were all over the door.
2. You left the refrigerator door open.
3. My half-eaten hot dog was on the table.
4. Clinging to the knife is mustard.
5. My mother saw the mess left by us.
6. The microwave is above the stove.
7. The window is glistening in the sun.
8. The soft curtains are blowing in the breeze.
9. We are fond of our kitchen.
10. My fantasy room is covered with posters.

Ending

Plan an ending to your paper just as you plan your beginning. For this paper you might want to make some comment upon the room, especially if this is one of the alternate topics. If you selected a messified room to describe, you might want to make a comment on what needs to be done. Whatever you decide upon, make sure the reader feels a sense of satisfaction and finality. Don't end with the words, "The End."

Before you begin to map out your ideas on the think sheet, read the two student models. The first student selected the messy kitchen as the topic in the essay entitled **The Disastrously Ravaged Kitchen**. The second student took a picture from a magazine as a topic.

The Disastrously Ravaged Kitchen

1. Toward the middle part of the west wall stands a **dining** table **covered** by a tablecloth **splattered** with egg yolks. 2. On the yellow-**painted** wall, violet grape juice stains stand out. 3. Muddy shoeprints cover the stairs **leading** out in the southeast corner of the room. 4. To the left of the stairs rests an open refrigerator **containing** spilled Coca Cola and milk, **mingling** in an open package of bologna. 5. On the stove to the left of the refrigerator, wiggly globs of Jello stick to the burners. 6. Several smelly pieces of ham plug up the electrical outlet above the stove. 7. Two feet away sits a counter top **cluttered** with **puddled** water and coffee grains. 8. An **overturned** blender adds to the mess. 9. Directly above the counter, a cabinet door hangs precariously by one hinge. 10. Chunks of wet bread and peanuts clog up the sink a few inches west of the **battered** cabinet. 10. The telephone, **torn** out of the wall, dangles by one wire to the left of the sink. This disastrous, terribly **ravaged** kitchen needs repair quickly!

Publisher's Note: Our students did not actually ravage the kitchen. However, an active imagination certainly is evident.

EXERCISE 5: Answer the following questions for the student models.

1. Does the first sentence locate the starting point?
2. What is the object the writer used?
3. Does the first sentence indicate the impression the writer is trying to create?

4. Is the paper organized spatially? (right to left, etc.)
5. Does the writer uses specific details in describing the objects in the room?
6. Could any of the descriptions of the objects been expanded to be more specific?
7. Could any empty words be subtracted?
8. What are the glue words used to show place?
9. Are there any dangling or misplaced modifiers because of ING action word beginnings?
10. Are all verbs in the present tense?
11. Are there any taboo words?
12. How did the paper end? Was it satisfactory?

Answer the questions above for the second student paper.

A Work Server Kitchen

1. A brick-**layed** fireplace on the left of the door in the center of the east wall brightens and warms the cheery room during the harsh winter months. 2. **Built** into the fireplace, a brick firewood holder supports a stack of chopped wood. 3. **Perched** on the mantlepiece above the fireplace, statues of ceramic seagulls rest. 4. **Opened** to let in the sunlight, white, lacy curtains blanket the tree-**paned, glistening** windows, which extend the entire length of the north wall. 5. Below the right drape stands a **colored**, floor-model television, pleasurably **used** every evening. 6. A brown and white **patterned** chair occupies the space a few feet left of the television. 7. The brass lamp with a white shade in front of the left drape sheds its **generated** light to the right upon a **matching**, cushioned, Hawaiian **designed** sofa. 8. Below the sofa lays a glass see-through table **containing** several magazines. 9. On the right side of the sofa stands an indoor **planted** palm tree. 10. A white shag rug carpets most of the brown **tiled** floor, **complimenting** the **paneled** walls. 11. A wood **carved** island **positioned** in the center of the room holds two bowls — one **containing** apples and the other **containing** fluffy, popped popcorn. 12. Four, four-**legged** bar stools surround this island, which serves as the kitchen table. 13. One of the room's two doorways extends to the west of the island. 14. A countertop stretches the length from the southwest to the southeast walls. 15. Several walnut **stained** cabinets hang over the counter. 16. Enclosed by a section of counter, a well-**supplied refrigerator on the south wall and an automatic dishwasher and sink on the southeast wall assist during the dinner hours. 17. Finally, a high-powered** microwave **sitting** to the east of the refrigerator also helps to display the easy life of this modern-day family. 18. Kitchens have certainly changed in the last few years.

Think Sheet

Your think sheet is a drawing of the area you have selected to describe. Complete your drawing think sheet as you are sitting in the room. If you decide to use a picture from a magazine, have that picture in front of you. If you decide to describe your fantasy room, visualize everything in its proper place.

List the objects that you intend to describe. Make them specific. Whenever possible, expand with ED word clusters.

Name _____ Period _____

SPATIAL DEVELOPMENT THINK SHEET

1. What is the object you are using as the starting point?
   _____

2. Where is this object located? _____

3. Write a tentative controlling idea. _____
   _____
   _____

4. Draw a rough sketch of your room, placing items in their proper place.

                              N

   W   E

                              S

5. On a separate sheet of paper, make a list of each object you intend to describe. Expand each object using descriptive words.

STAGE TWO: WRITING THE FIRST DRAFT

With your map think sheet in front of you, write your first draft. Do not be concerned with taboo words on your first draft. Just get the content on paper. Remember to skip lines and number sentences.

Here are some things to remember:

1. Begin with a controlling idea that names the object as a starting point. Locate that object using specific direction words. (northwest wall, southeast corner, etc.)
2. Organize your ideas spatially, left to right, etc.
3. Supply specific descriptions of the objects.
4. Link your ideas using place or locator glue words.
5. Keep the verbs in PRESENT tense.
6. Avoid ING action word openings.
7. End with some flare.

NOW WRITE YOUR FIRST DRAFT! Reread it carefully and circle the main verbs.

Sentence Opening Sheet

Here are the symbols to put above each column on the Sentence Opening Sheet:

DM-"ING action words" VAR-to the right	ED-EN words	VAR, VP Present S-V	VAR, RO
First Four Words	Special	Verbs	# of words per sentence

Now that your first draft is completed and the Sentence Opening Sheet filled out, check each column for the following:

Column One   **First Four Words**

1. Do all my sentences begin with directions such as "To the right," "To the left?" Can I rearrange some of them to make them more interesting?
2. Do any of my sentences begin with ING action words? Are those sentences introduced by dangling modifiers (DM)?

Column Two   **Special**

1. Did I use place glue word to indicate location of items? (See the list on page 82.)

Column Three   **Verbs**

1. Are all the verbs in the present tense?
2. Did I repeat the same verbs over and over again? (See the list on page 82.)
3. Do all the singular verbs (-S form) have singular subjects?

Column Four   **Number of Words Per Sentence**

1. Are any of my longer sentences run-ons?
2. Is there variety in my sentence lengths?

STAGE THREE: REWRITING

Before you exchange papers for a peer edit, criticize this model as a group activity. Use your checklist sheet or questions from Exercise 5 as your guide. Refer to the proofreading marks on page 158 to note mechanical errors.

The Mess

1. Looking into the kitchen, a grape jelly-smudged refrigerator stands along the south wall with its door wide open. 2. Under the windows dirty water spills from an overflowing sink, clogged with half slices of bread, hard-boiled eggs, a chocolate milk carton, and ten bottletops. 3. To the left of the sink stands a counter top, which is six feet long. 4. On top of it's surface sits peanut butter covered knives, four half-emptied jelly jars, and sausage. 5. Which is smeared with mayonnaise and marshmallow fluff. 6. Directly above on the wall, mustard and ketchup stains mingle with bubble gum. 7. Moving around the corner, a gallon milk carton

lied on its side, dripping moo juice onto a banana-smeared floor.
8. In the middle of this wall rest a food cabinet with one of its door hanging from its hinges. 9. Two doors in the middle of the southwest corner reveal a broom closet in which two empty tuna fish cans have been thrown. 10. It is easy to see that this room needs a major cleaning job.

SUPPLEMENTAL EXERCISE: This exercise contains errors in subject-verb agreement and dangling modifiers. To check for errors in subject-verb agreement, (S-V), first find the verb and ask, "What is it that rests, sits, stands, etc?" If the verb ends in "s," then there should be only one "what." If the verb does not end in "s," there should be more than one "what."

EXAMPLE: Walking through the door, a brown puddle of root beer cover a black heel mark left on the wooden floor.

Does it sound as though the puddle of root beer walks through the door? This is a dangling modifier.

The verb is "cover." Following the rule above, the what should be more than one. "Puddle" answers the question, so the subject and the verb do not agree in number.

REWRITTEN: A brown puddle of root beer covers a black heel left on the wooden floor.

1. Gazing down the table, an egg-shaped ham platter drip with milk.
2. Looking to the left, a coat drape over a golden floor lamp.
3. Soda bottletops blocks the water from going down the sink.
4. Draining in the sink, the oily pots and pans stinks from left over, burnt French fries.
5. Skipping down the table, a finger-smudged, gravy-smothered turkey platter sit unattended.
6. Eating quickly, the messy dishes are placed near the sink by the gang.
7. Scanning the room, a pile of dishes fills the sink.
8. To the right of the doorway stand a self-cleaning stove, cluttered with dirty pans on top of the burners.
9. Being messy and full of dirty dishes, the milk cartons lines up on top of the butcher block counter.
10. Above the kitchen stove hang a Chinese ornament with a White Sox cap dangling from the monster's tail.

Peer Evaluation Using a Checklist Sheet

Exchange papers with a proofreading partner. Read the paper two or three times so you understand the content. Before filling out the checklist sheet, draw your partner's room according to the description. Then compare your drawing with the writer's think sheet. The results might be interesting!

Writer's Name _____

Corrector's Name _____

SPATIAL DEVELOPMENT CHECKLIST

1. On a separate sheet of paper, draw a map of the writer's room. Then compare your drawing with the original think sheet.

2. Does the writer locate one object as a starting point? What is that object, and where is it located?

3. Is the paper organized spatially, from left to right, etc? If not, offer some suggestions.

4. How many objects did the writer include in the description?

5. Could the writer make any of these objects more interesting by expanding with ED words or clusters or other descriptive words? Make suggestions.

6. Circle the glue words use to help locate the objects. If more are necessary, mark this on the first draft.

7. Are all the verbs in the present tense? Are any taboo words present? If so, mark them.

8. Does the writer repeat the same verbs over and over again?

9. Does the writer have any dangling or misplaced modifiers because the sentences begin with ING action words? Mark them.

10. How does the paper end? Is it satisfactory?

11. Does the writer have any errors in subject-verb agreement? If so, mark them.

12. Mark all mechanical errors.

UNIT SEVEN PERSONAL OBSERVATION PAPER

In the **Personal Narrative** unit you told a story from the first person point of view. You used the pronouns "I," "we," "us," "my," "mine," "me," "our," and "ours." In this unit you will narrate a story about somebody else. This paper will be written in the third person point of view.

STAGE ONE: PREWRITING

Student Learning Objectives

1. The student will write a personal observation, using third person personal pronouns.
2. The student will use ING words to show motion and activity.
3. The student will organize the observation in a chronological sequence.
4. The student will link ideas using third person pronouns and/or time glue words.
5. The student will plunge into the action of the observation or write a general statement of the theme of the story.
6. The student will end with a clincher sentence.

Helpful Drills

In this paper you will be concentrating on ING words, present participles and gerunds. Since you will be writing about an action, ING words are good to use because they convey the sense of movement and activity. Here are some examples:

1. **Dashing** down the steps, Fernando reached into his pocket for his lunch money.
2. Melanie, **grasping** the tray of hamburgers and pop, cautiously carried it to the cashier.
3. **Biting** into a juicy bratwurst sandwich relieved my hunger pains for the time being.
4. Karen enjoys **skiing** down Mt. Bachelor more than anything in the world.

In the first two examples, the ING words are used as adjectives (present participles). "Dashing" describes Fernando. "Grasping" describes Melanie. In sentences three and four, the ING words are used as nouns (gerunds). Can you tell the difference between the ING words used as adjectives and as nouns?

ING words are also used as verbs when they accompany a helping verb such as: is, are, was, were, has been, had been.

Here are some examples:

1. The potatoes **were boiling** in the big kettle.
2. The balloonist **was sailing** peacefully across the blue sky.

However, you must be careful you do not confuse ING words as verbs when the helping word is missing. In this case they are adjectives. If you are not careful, fragments could result.

Here are some examples:

1. The potatoes **boiling** in the big kettle.
2. The balloonist **sailing** peacefully across the blue sky.

In the examples directly above, the ING words are used as adjectives; a fragment results. One way to correct the fragment would be to expand the sentence.

1. The potatoes boiling in the big kettle **would be used as the vegetable for a corned beef dinner.**
2. The balloonist sailing peacefully across the blue sky **enjoyed one of the happiest moments in her life.**

In this **Personal Observation** paper we want you to use ING words as adjectives and nouns. Consequently, you will be given a list of taboo words. These taboo verbs are the helping verbs needed for ING words to become verbs.

EXERCISE 1: Rearrange the following word groups by subtracting "empty" words. Eliminate all uses of "is," "are," "was," and "were." Write ING and ED word endings without writing fragments. Expand when necessary.

EXAMPLE: The student WHO WAS daydreaming jumped at the of the bell WHICH WAS ringing.

REWRITTEN: The **daydreaming** student jumped at the sound of the **ringing** bell.

"Daydreaming" and "ringing" are used as adjectives.

EXAMPLE: The mongrel WHO WAS barking and WHO WAS chasing the speeding car.

REWRITTEN: The **barking** mongrel **chasing** the speeding car (EXPAND) **smashed into the parked car.**

1. The bell WHICH WAS ringing WAS announcing the end of the class WHICH WAS the girls' gym.
2. The boys WHO WERE standing around and WHO WERE finished dressing WERE sent into a state of mass hysteria.
3. The sounds of the doors WHICH WERE locker doors WHICH WERE banging and WHICH WERE clanging and WHICH WERE slamming WERE echoing throughout the room WHICH the students WERE evacuating.
4. The junior high students WERE throwing their clothes together with their books and WERE making a mad dash for the mirror.
5. The eighth graders WHO WERE looking sloppy and WHO WERE pushing and WHO WERE shoving to get in front of the mirror.
6. The wall WHICH WAS bare had the mirror WHICH the girls WERE using to comb their hair.
7. The students WHO WERE opening the door and WHO WERE smelling the clean, fresh air WHICH WAS replacing the odor of the locker room WHICH WAS musty.
8. People WHO WERE in the hall and WHO WERE lazily resting against the gym doors.
9. The siren WHICH WAS blaring WAS giving them the signal to run for their lives.
10. Suddenly sixty gymnasts WHO WERE stampeding and WHO could be mistaken for animals WHICH WERE wild and WERE rushing through the door WERE creating chaos in the corridor.

EXERCISE 2: Eliminate the taboo words "is," "are," "was," and "were" in the following sentences. Combine and/or expand to write complete sentences instead of fragments:

EXAMPLE Sherman Shankley WAS chasing Wally Knucks down the hall.
Sherman skipped and broke his big toe.

REWRITTEN: Sherman Shankley, chasing Wally Knucks down the hall, slipped and broke his big toe.

SPECIAL PUNCTUATION RULE: If the ING phrase (participial phrase) supplies extra information not essential to the meaning of the sentence, set it off by commas. If the ING phrase supplies essential information, no commas are needed.

The girl standing on the pier is my cousin Judy.

Morgan Smothers, carrying the diploma, stepped from the stage.

1. Bulging Bennie WAS tackling the bank robber for the police. Bulging Bennie held him three hours.
2. Angel Belch WAS kicking the football. He scored the winning field goal.
3. The wild youngsters WERE looking at the storefront windows. They bought three AM-FM stereo radios.
4. Mr. Futinthemudd IS encouraging his students to study for the exam. He promised to buy all of them a McDonald's Big Mac.
5. Greasy Gert IS fixing today's pizza in the school cafeteria. She lit up a big, black cigar.
6. Fred WAS babysitting for his aunt. He finished all his homework.
7. Ozie WAS playing th biblical character David. He won the applause of the audience.
8. Big Paul WAS chopping down a tree. He used a new axe that his father had given to him for his birthday.
9. Clem WAS dancing the boogaloo. His belt broke.
10. Liz WAS running down the corridor. She bumped into Dean.

Subject

The purpose of this paper is for you to tell a story about some incident you observed. You should write about a person as he or she performs a series of actions to accomplish some goal. The observation could come from something you saw at school, at home, at the local park, on television, or at the movies. In fact, you could write about something that happened to you. Maybe you experienced tremendous joy in opening a special gift, sorrow in receiving some bad news, or frustration in not being chosen a cheerleader. Even if you select a personal experience, you must write this paper in the third person point of view. The pronouns you will use are:

THIRD PERSON PRONOUNS: he, she, it, they, them, their, his her, hers, him

In writing this personal observation, you should limit the time for your story. For example, if you decide to write about one observation from the movie **E.T.**, you might select Elliot's meeting with E.T. for the first time instead of providing a summary of the complete movie.

The choice of the subject is yours. Here are some suggested topics to get you thinking:

1. A boy holding a girl's hand for the first time
2. A teenager trying to get a loan from his folks
3. A student trying to get into the cafeteria line
4. A person buying a bratwurst at a crowded stand
5. Parents greeting a son or daughter coming home after curfew
6. An accident: skating, bicycling, roller skating, skiing
7. An exciting moment in a favorite movie or TV show
8. An incident on a vacation or camping trip
9. The most exciting event you observed in a sporting event
10. A friend opening a special gift you gave him or her

As a group activity, start brainstorming about some possible topics. Someone in your class might trigger an idea you can use for your topic.

After selecting a topic, ask yourself some key questions:

Why is this observation important?
What happened first? What was the atmosphere like?
What was the second thing that happened? How did the atmosphere change?
What actions did the character(s) perform that reveal inner feelings?
What happened next?
How did the incident end? Did the atmosphere change?

Controlling Idea

You have a few choices in the beginning of the observation. First, since observations provide an excellent way to point out a good idea, you might write a general statement of the theme of the story. Here are some examples:

Babysitting three youngsters under five years old can be a hair-raising experiece.

A practical joker can often become the butt of his own jokes.

Your second choice is to plunge immediately into the action of the story. Here is an example from a student composition about a a young boy challenging a video game:

Slowly Sammy shuffled up to the television. He flexed his fingers as if to start the blood circulating . . .

Organizing the Paper

Organize your ideas in a chronological time sequence. Begin with the main character's first action. Add feelings to the character. Remember, as a writer using the third person point of view, you have the power to get inside your character and write about what he or she feels.

Then write about the second action, etc. Think of the specific details to make your story interesting. Don't just recount the events. Describe the character's feelings and describe the atmosphere of the setting. Use your imagination!

Gluing Together Ideas

Besides using time glue words, you may also repeat pronouns and key words to link ideas together. Make sure your reader knows to whom the pronouns refer. After you use the character's name, switch to a pronoun, and then back to the name.

TIME GLUE WORDS: first, then, now, suddenly, later, finally, second, again, etc.

EXERCISE 3: Read the sample composition below. Substitute pronouns for the character's name whenever necessary.

Root'em on to a Big Victory

1. Gulping down Clyde Cresslily's root beer and piggishly spilling half of Clyde Cressliy's buttered popcorn in Clyde Cresslily's lap, Clyde Cresslily pounded Clyde Cresslily's fist on the grandstand seat and shouted out some half-witted cheers while the Slippery Rock Aeros started a rally in the bottom of the tenth. 2. Jumping up and down at the sight of a triple, Clyde Cresslily shook the elderly lady sitting next to Clyde

Cresslily back and forth as two runs scored. 3. Jumping for joy as the winning run crossed the plate, Clyde Cresslily tore Clyde Cresslily's empty popcorn box into tiny pieces and threw the confetti into the air to show Clyde Cresslily's delight at the outcome of the game. 4. After waiting for the crowd to clear away, Clyde Cresslily flashed a victory smile to the shortstop and wished the shortstop luck in tomorrow's game.

Taboo Words (Teacher option)

Try to use ING words as adjectives and nouns in this paper. Consequently, you should avoid using verb helpers such as "is," "are," "was," and "were." Remember, you practiced subtracting these words in the helpful drills. Also, if you write this paper in the third person point of view, you will want to avoid shifting reference. Avoid using first and second person pronouns, "you know."

Here is a list of taboo words: is, are, was, were

Ending

The ending should be part of the overall strategy. You might end with a sense of finality by the main character's accomplishing the original goal. You may also end by making some comment on the meaning of this event. Whatever you decide, make sure you do not end with the statement "The End" or some other statement that tells the reader the story is over such as, "And that ended the incident."

Student Models

Before you begin to work on your think sheet, read the following student personal observations. Use these questions as your guide.

1. What is the observation being written about?
2. How is it limited in time, space, characters, and action?
3. How did the writer begin the observation? By plunging into the action or beginning with a thematic statement controlling idea?
4. Are the events in a time sequence?
5. Did the writer skip any key actions?

6. Are the ideas specific? Does the writer let us feel what the main character experiences?
7. Did the writer use pronouns or time glue words to shift between actions?
8. Are all verbs in the same tense?
9. Does the writer use ING words to convey motion or activity?
10. How did the paper end?

The Pinball Wizard

1. As the pinball wizard casually walked into the game room, he reached into the pocket of his faded blue jeans to pull out a quarter. 2. He first checked the coin return cup for some money, which might have been forgotten by a forgetful person, and then he examined his quarter for defects, and with his delicate fingers, he slid it into the coin slot on the front of the pinball machine. 3. While waiting for the score register to reset itself to zero, he shuffled his feet trying to find a comfortable position for standing. 4. Before starting to play, he opened a can of pop, which he lifted to his lips and took a sip. 5. After placing the can on the floor, he grasped the knob which shoots the ball, and after pulling the knob back to the desire length, he released it sending the ball into a field of flashing lights and ringing bells. 6. Reflected images of silver spheres appeared in the pinball wizard's eyes as he gazed at the ball. 7. With split-second accuracy, he pushed the flipper button, hurling the silver ball back into the ringing and flashing field. 8. His fancy footwork caused him to kick the can of pop, which toppled over. 9. His wrists kept flexing as he pushed the flipper buttons, allowing him to score more points. 10. A loud thud from the machine indicated that the pinball wizard scored a replay and once again defeated the mechanical monster.

Don't Take My Spoon

1. Wendy lay in her crib, content with her most prized possession, a blue plastic spoon. 2. Suddenly, out of nowhere, came a huge hand that whisked it away. 3. Outraged, Wendy decided to let the world know of this offending action. 4. Slowly but surely, her frustrated frown turned into a pouting, drawn-out grimace. 4. With her muscles tense, she clenched her fists and let out a furious high-pitched screech. 5. A waterfall of tears gushed down her face, making tiny streams run down her neck. 6. Enraged that anyone would dare touch her spoon, Wendy's shocked face burned bright red. 7. Her screams grew louder. 8. She jumped up and down in the crib. 9. After a few minutes, Wendy's pained expression finally convinced her brother that the spoon was absolutely necessary for peace in the house. 9. He threw it back into Wendy's crib, and her frown turned into a wide smile.

The Big Play

1. The outcome of the 1967 NFL championship game between the Green Bay Packers and the Dallas Cowboys depended on the last crucial play of the game. 2. In the bitter cold Dallas scarcely led the Packers 17-14 with only 16 seconds left in the game. 3. With the Packers having the ball on the goal line, Bart Starr, their quarterback, called a time-out. 4. After trotting over to the sidelines, he talked over the strategy for the next play with coach Vince Lombardi. 5. The defensive captain for the Cowboys ran over to his sidelines and discussed strategy with his coach, Tom Landry. 6. Meanwhile, thousands of bundled-up fans froze as they peered down on the icy field anxiously waiting the play to begin. 7. On the goal line a tight circle of referees stood talking and waiting nervously in the below zero weather. 8. Bundled players on both sidelines danced and rubbed their hands trying to fight the cold. 9. All of a sudden, Bart Starr trotted onto the field. 10. He appeared to be ready. 11. The Packers huddled and Starr called the simplest play in football, the quarterback sneak. 12. Since Starr planned to go over to the right guard, everything depended on a solid block from Jerry Kramer. 13. Thousands of people in the stadium and millions at home watched as the Packers broke the huddle and lined up in position. 14. The Cowboys dug in their cleats, ready to charge, in the frozen turf. 15. Barking out the signals, Bart Starr took the snap. 16. Kramer plunged low into Jethro Pugh, and Starr dove over the goal line holding the ball as tightly as possible. 17. After checking if Starr still held the ball, the referee raised his arms signaling a touchdown. 18. Packer fans screamed hysterically as others stood in awe. 19. The Packers jumped around hugging each other as the Cowboys walked dejectedly off the field. 20. Green Bay had won the most exciting finish in pro football history.

Think Sheet

Now explore your topic to see if you can remember enough information about it. Your think sheet serves as a concrete way of your recounting the events of your observation.

Some of your think sheets might be duplicated for class discussion purposes. Others might be shared in small group discussions.

Try to visualize what happened.

Name _____ Period _____

PERSONAL OBSERVATION THINK SHEET

1. What goal was the character trying to accomplish? _____
   _____
2. How long did the action take place? _____
3. Where did it take place? _____
4. How many participants? _____
5. List the specific actions necessary to accomplish the goal. Use these helpful questions as you jot down your ideas.

   What specific actions did the character perform to accomplish the goal?
   What physical actions reveal the character's inner feelings?
   What were the surroundings? How did they affect the character?
   What events came before the main action? Did they influence the character?
   What was the character's mental state at the beginning? What indicated this?
   What do the character's clothing and mannerisms, etc., reveal about him/her?

Glue Words	List the Actions	What are the Specific Details
_____	1st	_____
_____	2nd	_____
_____		_____
_____		_____
_____		_____
_____		_____
_____		_____
_____		_____
_____	Last	_____

SPECIAL HINT: In writing your first draft, include inner feelings of the character's doing the action. Use only third person pronouns. (he, his, him, her, hers, they, them, their)

STAGE TWO: WRITING THE FIRST DRAFT

Write your first draft with your think sheet in front of you. If you decide to include dialogue in your paper, refer to the rules for punctuation on pages 68 and 69.

Here are some things to remember:

1. Plunge immediately into the action of the story or provide a general thematic statement CI.
2. Organize the ideas in a time sequence.
3. Include specific details with the character's action. As a writer using third person pronouns, you have the power to tell your reader the feelings of the main character(s).
4. Use ING action words whenever possible.
5. Keep the verbs in the same tense. If writing about an incident that happened in the past, it will be easier to use past tense. However, if you want the reader to feel as if he/she is observing the incident as it is happening, use present tense verbs.
6. End with some sense of finality. The goal is completed. The observation is over.

NOW WRITE YOUR FIRST DRAFT! Reread it carefully and circle the main verbs.

Sentence Opening Sheet

Here are the symbols to put above each column on the Sentence Opening Sheet.

VAR, FRAG	ING words "you"	Tense, VP VAR	RO VAR # of words
First Four Words	Special	Verbs	per sentence

Now that your first draft is completed and the Sentence Opening Sheet is filled out, check each column for the following:

Column One   **First Four Words**

1. Do I begin each sentence with the main character's name?
2. Are any of my sentences fragments because they begin with glue words? **HINT:** Reread your composition backwards one sentence at a time.

Column Two   **Special**

1. Did I shift references by using first and second person pronouns, the taboo words for this paper?
   *In column two, you might have listed words like "you," "you know," or "I."
2. Did I use ING words to show action and movement? If you notice you do not have any ING words in this column, you might want to include some as you combine and rearrange some sentences.

Column Three   **Verbs**

1. Are all my verbs in the same tense?
2. Did I repeat the same verbs over and over again?
3. Did I include any taboo verbs?

Column Four   **Number of Words Per Sentence**

1. Can I combine any short, choppy sentences to make them more interesting?
2. Are any overly long sentences run-ons?

After checking over the Sentence Opening Sheet, make your corrections of the first draft.

STAGE THREE: REWRITTING

Before you exchange papers, read over the sample student first draft. It might help you to identify similar errors in your own paper. Use your checklist sheet or questions for the student models on pages 99 – 100 as your guide. Refer to the proofreading marks on page 158 to note mechanical errors.

Never Again

1. Patty gazed over the steep, snow covered slope. 2. She now had second thoughts about skiing down the hill. 3. Although she had already accepted the challenge. 4. As she glances at the big bumps and the icy spots, she began to lose her courage. 5. Holding the poles tightly, Patty dug them into the snow she pushed off and started her run down the hill. 6. Blowing against her face, the cold wind caused her eyes to tear. 7. She has a difficult time seeing as she began to pick up speed. 8. She panicked. 9. She tried to remember what the ski instructor had told her about slowing down. 10. She flew off the ground as she hit a big bump. 11. Her arms became extended she lost control of everything. 12. She prays as she tumbled over and over. 13. Finally, she came to a complete stop. 14. Feeling helpless, Patty decides to go the bunny slope before she tries the big hill again.

SUPPLEMENTAL EXERCISE: The following sentences have fragment errors caused by ING, WH, and glue words. Rewrite them to eliminate the errors. **HINT:** Expand!

1. The policeman who was swinging his nightstick. He stood on the corner.
2. The old Chevy which was packed with teenagers. The Chevy had a broken left headlight.
3. Quarterback Joe Gentry faded back for the pass. As the end broke from the line of scrimmage.
4. When the whistle sounded. The girls rushed to the locker room.
5. The ambulance which had a loud siren which was blaring. The ambulance rushed the ballet dancer to the emergency room.
6. Opening the window, Harvey Wallhanger carrying his Colt .45.
7. Louise is the only one. Who knew the address of Anthony's Diner.
8. At Great America Amusement Park Eric found the wallet. Which belonged to his brother Mark.
9. Mildred enjoys sleeping all day. After frying hamburgers at Prince's Burger Palace all night long.
10. The unhappy student searching in her purse for her student identification card.

Peer Evaluation Using a Checklist Sheet

Exchange papers with a proofreading partner. Read the paper two or three times so you understand the content. Then answer the questions on the Checklist Sheet.

Writer's Name _____

Corrector's Name _____

PERSONAL OBSERVATION CHECKLIST

1. What is the observation the writer is describing?

2. Did the writer plunge into the action of the story or was a controlling idea provided?

3. Was the opening interesting? Why or why not? If not, offer some suggestions.

4. How long does the story take place?

5. Is the paper organized in a time sequence?

6. Are there any gaps? Are there any places that need to be expanded? Mark them on the first draft.

7. Does the writer supply specific feelings of the main character? If not, mark the spot(s) on the first draft and offer some suggestions.

8. Does the writer use glue words and/or pronouns to link ideas?

9. How did the paper end?

10. Does the writer use ING words to convey motion and activity?

11. Are all the verbs in the same tense? Did the writer use any taboo verbs?

12. Did the writer use any first or second person pronouns? Mark them on the first draft.

13. Do any of the sentences need to be combined to make them more interesting?

14. Mark all mechanical errors.

UNIT EIGHT   LISTING PAPER

One of the easiest ways to increase organization is to make lists: shopping, repairs, homework assignments, etc. In this paper you will use your list making skills to prove a point.

STAGE ONE: PREWRITING

Student Learning Objectives

1. The student will write a controlling idea that states the subject and arouses reader interest.
2. The student will organize the paper by enumerating ideas.
3. The student will use reasons, facts, or examples to support the subject.
4. The student will use glue words to link ideas.
5. The student will practice eliminating the forms of the verbs "to be," "to have," "to do," and "to get."
6. The student will end the paper with either the last item on the list or a statement which makes a final comment on the subject.

Helpful Drills

When a writer wants to prove something to a reader, careful attention must be paid to the words chosen. In particular, the verbs used must convey verb power. Before working on the first draft, practice substituting specific verbs for general ones in the following exercises.

A good way to develop VERB POWER is to substitute more specific words for the general ones being used. The verbs "be," "do," "have," and "get" are the basic predicates in the English language. All other verbs are a more specified form of these. For example, "Nikki is happy" can be rewritten "Nikki jumps for joy." When you substitute for the forms of "to be," you must expand the original idea and use an action word that shows the condition being written about. "To be happy" becomes "jumps for joy." The latter gives the reader a clear picture of what is being described.

When you substitute for forms of "to do," the noun can become the verb. You worked on some of these exercises in UNIT ONE. "Ringo does his laundry in the wash tub" can be rewritten "Ringo

WASHED his laundry in the wash tub." "To do the wash" becomes either "to wash the laundry or to launder."

When you substitute for the forms of "to have," use an action word that clearly describes what the subject is doing. For example, the sentence, "Ezzard has a strong arm" can be rewritten "Ezzard's throw knocked Sunny over." By expanding and substituting an action verb, the reader knows just how strong Ezzard's arm really is.

Finally, when you substitute for forms of "to get," you eliminate an overused but empty verb. In the sentence "Aleka gets my morning newspaper," "gets" can be replaced by a number of more colorful verbs such as "retrieves," "fetches," "grasps," or "recovers." This verb is the easiest of the four powerless verbs to eliminate because a short trip to the thesaurus can yield a number of suitable replacements.

Here is a list of the forms of the verbs "to be," "to do," "to have," and "to get."

TO BE: is, are, was, were, has been, had been, will be, will have been
TO DO: do, did, done, does
TO HAVE: have, has, had
TO GET: get, gets, got

EXERCISE 1: Rewrite the following sentences eliminating the "to be," "to do," "to have," and "to get" verbs. Try to use no new verb more than once. Remember, EXPAND! Do a few together as a class first.

EXAMPLE: The cat **is** in the window.

REWRITTEN: The cat **lounges** in the warm, sunny window.

EXAMPLE: Pat **does** the floors.

REWRITTEN: Pat **waxes** the floors as a part-time job.

1. Scott John is a great musician.
2. Jessica is quiet.
3. Ginger was always sad.
4. The Wychs are a hard-working family.
5. Uncle Clarence is a story teller.
6. Donald did a term paper.
7. Cassie does the dishes every evening.
8. Kevin did his homework just before class.
9. Marcella did her nails.

10. Carlos does well in soccer.
11. Mario has a new car.
12. Larry has a nice cottage.
13. The Peters have friendly smiles.
14. Raymond has a tough job.
15. Wilma had a good time in Bagdad.
16. Sara got up at seven.
17. Mr. Waters couldn't get an expensive meal.
18. Sheila always gets candy for a gift.
19. Stephen got jam on the floor.
20. Joni tried to get an education.
21. Javier is in the front row.
22. The doctor did an examination.
23. Mexico has nice beaches.
24. The child got the mumps.
25. Computers are fun.
26. Patsy is a zookeeper.
27. Martina has a pretty smile.
28. The plane didn't fly.
29. He hasn't been to Alaska.
30. This will be the last sentence.

EXERCISE 2: Because you will be asked to list reasons, facts, and examples to support or prove a particular point, this might be a good time for the class to practice brainstorming for those items on a sample subject. As a class, see how many reasons, facts, and examples you can add to the list below to support allowing a one month winter holdiay.

EXAMPLE USING REASONS:
1. Worst weather during late December, early January
2. Holiday season demands family gatherings

Subject

A listing paper is one in which the writer lists reasons, facts, and examples to support a point on a particular subject. In this paper you should select a topic which can be proven by listing six or seven proofs of your general idea. Many kinds of subjects lend themselves to this type of organization. Whenever you present information on any subject, you could use the listing method. Science, social studies, and, of course, literature papers are naturals for this method.

Several suggested topics are listed below. However, if you would rather select a subject of your own choice, ask your teacher for approval.

Suggested Topics

1. At _____ Junior High School, the rule concerning _____ should be eliminated from the student handbook.
2. Seventh and/or eighth graders use their own jargon.
3. (ANY PARTICULAR WORKING GROUP) has its own jargon: doctors, nurses, lawyers, policemen, construction workers, baseball players, show business people, band members, etc.
4. There are many useless gadgets in today's car/kitchen.
5. Some of today's teenage clothing causes people to stop and stare.
6. Wendy's is better for hamburgers than Burger King. (Use any restaurant names.)
7. Imagine you have just won the million dollar lottery. What gifts would you buy your family and friends?
8. Choose an important person in your community such as the mayor, council member, senator, representative, etc., and explain why he/she is a good or bad representative of the people.
9. Think about the last book you read. Tell why someone would or would not want to read it.
10. Tell why it is best/worst to have brothers and/or sisters.
11. _____ is the best place to go for summer (or any other season) vacation.
12. _____ is a fun hobby.

Controlling Idea

The controlling idea, usually the first sentence in this type of paper, should state your opinion about the subject. It includes the subject and key words that will be proven or defended by your listing of reasons, facts, and/or examples.

SAMPLE CONTROLLING IDEA: If winter vacation lasted one month instead of two weeks, both students and teachers would benefit.

Organizing The Paper

After you have selected the subject and written the controlling idea, jot down four or five specific reasons, facts, and examples to prove your CI. Refer back to Exercise 2 for brainstorming tips. If you are going to use facts, make sure your information is correct.

Since this is a listing paper, your ideas will not follow a definite order. However, you should try to have some strategy in planning your outline. Your ideas should be written in the order you feel will have the most impact upon the reader.

Later in writing your first draft, add specific details that are not included in your tentative outline (think sheet), so you are supplying more evidence to support your controlling idea. Be as specific as you can. Expand!

Gluing Together Ideas

In this paper you must be extremely careful to glue ideas together. The reader must not become confused when one proof ends and another begins. To help you link together ideas, glue words are listed below.

GLUE WORDS: Also, another, besides, furthermore, moreover, in addition, again.

Think of other words used to indicate a shift of ideas.

Ending

Your ending should be part of your overall planning. You may end on the last item of the enumeration, or you may make a comment on the meaning of your proofs. Whatever ending you decide upon, make sure you spend time thinking about it. The ending should leave the reader convinced your point of view has some merit. Finally, give your paper a title which gives the reader a hint about your paper.

EXERCISE 3: Before writing your first draft, study the sample composition. Use the questions which follow as a guide for class discussion.

Crazy Laws

1. The city council of Spittville, Ohio, needs to eliminate some of its outdated laws. 2. In a section labeled "promotion of marriage," an ordinance makes it unlawful for anyone to take money for arranging a marriage. 3. According to city ordinance 99, section 9, "All weeks are hereby declared to be a public nuisance." 4. The law penalizes anyone who releases pigeons in the seventh ward. 5. Taking a cigarette butt out of a public ashtray with the intent to sell also incurs a fine. 6. Fortune tellers or anyone who rollerskates on city streets faces immediate arrest. 7. Children even feel the pinch of crazy laws because they most obtain a permit to jump or play hopscotch on a city sidewalk. 8. Also, if children beg for money on any street for any reason, they face arrest. 9. Obviously, ignored by all Spittvillians, these outdated and humorous laws require elimination.

1. What is the controlling idea of the paper?
2. What are the key words the writer must prove?
3. How many items did the writer use to support the controlling idea?
4. How could you make each idea more specific?
5. Which items were reasons? Facts? Examples?
6. Did the writer supply enough proofs?
7. How were the ideas glued together?
8. Were the verb tenses consistent?
9. How did the paper end?

(**NOTE:** Sentence 3 contains the taboo words "are" and "to be." In this case the usage is permitted as the writer quotes the specific city ordinance.)

Think Sheet

Your think sheet is a natural listing of the reasons, facts, examples, or statistics that support your subject. It enables you to check to see if you know enough about your subject. If you find yourself having difficulty listing enough evidence about a particular subject, it would be a good time to either do additional thinking or switch topics.

After you complete your think sheet, your teacher might want to duplicate a volunteer copy for class discussion purposes. In fact, you might want to exchange think sheets with a classmate to check for specific ideas.

Name _____ Period _____

A LISTING PAPER THINK SHEET

1. What is the subject of this paper? Select the subject from your own experience. _____

2. Jot down all the specific reasons, facts, examples, or statistics that support your subject. Also, list appropriate glue words.

Proof – Specific Details	glue words
A.	
B.	
C.	
D.	
E.	
F.	
G.	

3. Tentative controlling idea _____
_____

HELPFUL HINT: Make sure your ideas are specific. In writing your first draft, organize your ideas in the order your feel will have the greatest impact upon your reader.

SUPER SPECIAL HINT: If you cannot list enough items on your think sheet, throw it away and start again. Maybe you don't know enough about your subject.

STAGE TWO: WRITING THE FIRST DRAFT

Have your think sheet in front of you as you write your first draft. Do not be concerned with taboo words (as listed above Exercise 1) on your first draft. Just get your ideas on paper. Make sure to skip lines and number your sentences.

Here are some things to remember:

1. Begin with the controlling idea that names your subject and key words.
2. Follow the organizational pattern you feel will impact your reader the most.
3. Expand each reason, fact, example, or statistic used. Use the journalistic questions if you find yourself having difficulty supplying specifics.
4. Link your ideas using enumeration glue words.
5. Keep your verbs in the same tense. (Past is easiest for this paper.)
6. End with a final item or statement about your subject.

NOW WRITE YOUR FIRST DRAFT! Reread it carefully and circle each main verb.

Sentence Opening Sheet

Here are the symbols to put above each column on the sentence opening sheet.

var frag	glue	past VP, Taboo	RO, var
first four words	special	verbs	# of words per sentence

Now that your first draft is completed and the sentence opening sheet is filled out, check each column for the following:

Column One   **First Four Words**

1. Do all of my sentences begin with the same word or sentence structure? Can I rearrange any of them to make them more interesting?
2. Do any of my sentences begin with glue words or ING words making them perhaps fragments?

Column Two   **Special**

1. Did I use enumeration glue words to link various items listed to prove my controlling idea?

Column Three   **Verbs**

1. Are all my verbs in the past tense?
2. Did I repeat the same verbs over and over again?
3. Did I use too many "to be," "to do," "to have," or "to get" verbs?

Column Four   **Number of Words Per Sentence**

1. Do any of my short, choppy sentences need to be combined to make them more interesting?
2. Are any of my longer sentences run-ons?

STAGE THREE: REWRITING

Before you exchange papers for a peer edit, criticize this sample first draft. Use your checklist sheet or the questions from Exercise 3 to help you find errors. Refer to proofreading marks on page 158 to note mechanical errors.

EXERCISE 4: Reread the questions from Exercise 3. Then as a group activity criticize this sample first draft. Give specific examples which could help the writer improve the paragraph. For example, sentence 1 has two taboo words, "are," and it repeats itself. You might even try rewriting one or two of the sentences as a class.

Pet Peeves

1. Pet Peeves are little things that bug you, and little things that bug you are pet peeves. 2. Everyone has these because they have

likes and dislikes. 3. One pet peeve I have is that I can't stand to babysit for free. 4. I also do not like it when I babysit and don't get paid until a month later. 5. Another pet peeve I have is I dislike getting in trouble with my teacher for not selling raffle books. 6. It's not fair because I couldn't sell mine because my parents went on a three week cruise and I had to stay with my Aunt Minny. 7. The last pet peeve I have is the location of my locker. 8. I am short, but I get a top locker. 9 The person who has the bottom locker is, you guessed it, tall. 10. These are just a few of my pet peeves that I mentioned in the controlling idea.

SUPPLEMENTAL SENTENCES: These sentences contain verb errors. The writer used weak forms of "to be," "to have," "to do," or "to get" instead of strong, action verbs. Rewrite each sentence using the skills of combination, rearrangement, subtraction, and expansion to eliminate the taboo words.

EXAMPLE: The computer **is** a helpful tool. It **can be** a great help to a writer.

REWRITTEN: Writers **find** the computer a helpful tool.

1. C.B.ers **have** their own jargon. It **is** to fool the highway patrolman.
2. A speedometer **is** not necessary because all one **has to do is** to look at the traffic flow and go no faster.
3. Winter vacation **is** when students get **to do** all the fun winter sports.
4. We all have things we like to do during December, and to get only two weeks is hard.
5. My brother, who is in college, gets almost six weeks off in the winter.
6. Doing homework is easy if one has an organized system.
7. When driving, seatbelts are most uncomfortable for driving.
8. A dishwasher is very useless, for it's an energy waster and the job can be done by hand.
9. Bowling can be fun when a person gets instructions on how to do it properly.
10. When the last ball has been rolled out and the last pin knocked over, the score can be totaled.

Peer Evaluation Using A Checklist Sheet

Exchange papers with a proofreading partner. Read his or her paper two or three times, so you understand the content before you answer the questions on the checklist sheet.

Writer's name _____

Corrector's name _____

LISTING CHECKLIST

1. Write out the controlling idea in the space provided.

2. What are the key words the writer must prove?

3. How many different reasons, facts, examples, or statistics did the writer include to prove the controlling idea? Number them on the first draft.

4. Does the writer supply enough support? If not, help expand by supplying some ideas of your own.

5. Circle all glue words. Add any where necessary to note a shift in proofs.

6. Check to see all verbs are in the same (past) tense.

7. Circle any taboo words - "to be," "to do," "to have," and "to get" verbs. Do too many taboo words weaken what the writer has written?

8. Indicate if any sentences should be combined or rearranged (**IMPACT**) to make them more interesting.

9. Check to see the writer did not repeat any unnecessary ideas.

10. What type of ending did the writer use? Could it be more effective?

11. Mark any mechanical and spelling errors you find.

UNIT NINE   ORDER OF IMPORTANCE PAPER

Every student has strong feelings about controversial topics. You ought to be able to support your opinion on one of these issues clearly and logically.

STAGE ONE: PREWRITING

Student Learning Objectives

1. The student will select a topic from his/her own personal experience.
2. The student will write a controlling idea that states his/her position on a controversial issue.
3. The student will organize the paper in either most important to least important or least important to most important idea order.
4. The student will use reasons, facts, examples, or statistics to support the subject.
5. The student will use glue words, WH-words, ING words, or ED words to combine ideas of unequal importance.
6. The student will write an ending to the paper which restates the controlling idea, summarizes all the supportive proofs, ends with the impact of the last argument, or makes a comment on the supportive proofs.

Helpful Drills

So far you have become competent in using the skills of combination, rearrangement, subtraction, and expansion. You have become selective in your choice of words. You have learned how to substitute for the weak "to be," "to do," "to get," and "to have" verbs. You have learned where to place main ideas. You have learned how to combine larger sentences and make ideas of greater importance stand out. Now that you have control over these basic writing techniques, use all of them to create a desired impact through smooth word flow. If your writing does not create impact upon the reader, it will be lifeless, unaccepted, and worthless.

EXERCISE 1: Rewrite the following sentences, putting the idea that creates the greatest impact in the main sentence. Use glue words, WH words, ING and ED words to introduce the lesser idea. As you rewrite these sentences, remain aware of the construction patterns and use a variety of combinations. Underline the main idea in each rewritten sentence.

EXAMPLE: Frank Patton retired from the Air Force. He achieved the rank of Brigadier General.

If the writer wished to stress the idea that Frank Patton retired from the Air Force, the sentence could be written in these ways:

Frank Patton who achieved the rank of Brigadier General **retired from the Air Force**.

or

Frank Patton retired from the Air Force after achieving the rank of Brigadier General.

If the writer wished to stress the idea that Frank Patton achieved the rank of Brigadier General, the sentence could be written in these ways:

Before retiring from the Air Force, **Frank Patton achieved the rank of Brigadier General.**

or

Frank Patton who retired from the Air Force **achieved the rank of Brigadier General.**

Note the location of the main ideas. Review comma rule 2 on page 15.

1. Slinging Sam is the hottest gunslinger in the West. He drew his Colt 45.
2. Paul Cahill is the author of **Gordon's Head.** He plays the "Official Baseball Game" in his spare time. He works for United Air Lines.
3. Stacey Barry is an excellent gymnast. She trains at Sandburg Junior High School.
4. Hot Wheels Willie drives a Triumph Spitfire. He won the Seattle 500 mile race in record time.
5. Quigley High has an excellent basketball team. They won the South Central Basketball League Championship.
6. Charley O. Rigley sells bubble gum. He owns a major league baseball team.
7. The audience sat on the edge of their seats. They bit their fingernails. They closed their eyes.

8. Jessica Barister studied diligently for the exam. She wanted to become a lawyer.
9. Kim Young walked up to the 18th tee. She placed the ball. She took some practice swings. She hit a hole in one.
10. The paramedic jumped into the ambulance. He started the motor, and he turned on the switch for the light. He turned on the siren, and he raced to the scene of the accident.

EXERCISE 2: "It's not fair" is often an argument given against some rule. As a class, think of an issue which affects you for which "it's not fair" could be used as an argument. Brainstorm all the possible arguments **for** the issue. Then using the previous arguments, see if you can counter all the for arguments with arguments **against** the issue. If you have out thought the opposition, you opinions will prevail.

Use the sample topic below, or another which is important to students in your class to practice the For-Against argument skill.

EXAMPLE: Students have to pay adult prices at the movie theater, yet they must be accompanied by an adult — or worse — they cannot see "R" rated movies. "It isn't fair!" As a group activity, brainstorm a list why this rule is fair. Then for every item for, come up with an argument why the rule isn't fair.

Subject

There are times when a writer must take a strong stance on an issue. He/she must either be for or against something, and he/she must have sufficient knowledge about the subject to write a believable argument. It takes more than an emotional feeling about the topic. It requires specific knowledge of reasons, facts, and examples to support the argument.

The purpose of this paper is to convince your reader of your opinion on a particular issue. Since you must be very familiar with the point you are going to prove and feel quite strongly about it, the choice of the subject will be left to you. A list of suggested topics follows. Use the list to choose a suitable topic or as a point of departure for your individual topic. In either case, make sure your topic is sufficiently limited to be convincingly argued for or against in a one paragraph paper.

Suggested Topics

1. Students should not receive homework over the weekend.
2. Teenage girls should have equal employment opportunities with teenage boys.
3. Girls' sports should receive the same dollar amount of support as boys' sports.
4. The school rule banning _____ should be abolished.
5. People under 16 years of age should not have to pay an adult price to see a movie.
6. My parents' rule about _____ should be relaxed.
7. Students should be allowed to turn in homework as late as they want.
8. A class in computer literacy should/should not be mandatory for high school graduation.
9. Sports figure _____ should be traded, benched, fired, etc.
10. Physical education should/should not be required in junior high school.
11. Seat belts should/should not be mandatory while driving.
12. Any current controversial school issue. (dress code, tardiness, lunchroom procedures, more pep assemblies, method of electing cheerleaders, etc.)

Controlling Idea

The controlling idea for this paper should be at the beginning. The key words should show the strong stance you will take in the paper. Before starting your controlling idea, some background information about the controversial issue should be given to the reader. In most cases, the writer is asking for a change or is against a change. Therefore, the background information could be a brief statement of the history leading up to the issue considered in the paper.

Two sample controlling ideas follow. The first idea simply states the subject and the key words. This would generally be the first sentence in the paragraph. The second sample shows another more advanced method of beginning a paragraph. The writer has chosen to use some background information before stating the subject and key words.

SAMPLE CONTROLLING IDEA: Students should be allowed to wear whatever they wish to school as long as it does not disrupt the learning or teaching process.

SAMPLE CONTROLLING IDEA: Physical fitness has become one of the most important ways to maintain health throughout one's life. Doctors point to a regular exercise program as one of the best ways to prevent heart attack. But physical fitness does not just happen, it begins in school. **Therefore, all students should take physical education throughout high school.**

The background information leads the reader with reasons to the controlling idea: why this person believes in the stance that all students should take physical education.

Organizing the Paper

After you have selected your topic, think about all the arguments which could be used against your opinion. By listing all the possible reasons why your opinion is weak, you can anticipate any gaps in your paper. Then, jot down all the reasons, facts, and examples which support your controlling idea. You should have at least one item to counter those opposing ideas. If you are not sure of all the exact proofs, don't be afraid to look up the information. Now, subtract the unnecessary items which might be considered emotional or inaccurate.

Before writing your first draft, arrange the ideas in a specific order of importance. If you organize your paper from the most to the least important idea, you are giving the beginning of your composition the greater impact. If you organize your paper from the least important to the most important, you are building the reader up for a climactic ending. Use one of these organizational patterns for this paper. Be sure to add exact and correct specific details when you write the first draft.

Here is list of ideas from a sample composition.

CONTROLLING IDEA: Although many people doubt and scoff at the idea, life does exist on planets other than earth.

Arguments Against:
1. Science fiction is just what it says, "fiction."
2. If we were not the only people in the universe, why haven't we heard from anyone yet?
3. People who write books about beings from outer space take coincidental happenings and try to draw connections between them.
4. Television programs about space are just the products of very vivid imaginations.
5. Scientific evidence about our own solar system shows life unable to exist anywhere other than our planet.

Arguments For:
1. UFO's spotted by members of Strategic Air Command.
2. Strange sounds from outer space.
3. Markings near Peru's Andes Mountains.
4. TV programs proving people live on other planets: "Star Trek," "Lost in Space," "Mork and Mindy," "V," etc.
5. Department stores selling ray guns and space suits.
6. Erik Von Daniken's book **Chariots of the Gods**.
7. Scientists discovering falling meteors.
8. Ancient storage battery found.
9. Peruvian Indians unable to make landing markings.
10. Millions of stars, planets, and galaxies.
11. Submarines penetrating the ocean floor.
12. Impossible that only the planet earth would be populated by people.

Which ideas from the above two lists could and should be subtracted?

Gluing Ideas Together

Glue words can be used to show the order of importance in linking ideas together. The writer must be sure the reader knows which ideas stand out in the writer's mind. Here is a list of glue words which indicate order of importance:

GLUE WORDS: also, another, besides, furthermore, moreover, in addition, again, first, second, third, finally, next, too, similarly, of primary importance, the most important, the most appealing, the least, the most, the greatest.

When the writer has determined which ideas are of greater importance, he/she can control the development of the argument for the reader.

EXERCISE 3: Glue words have been subtracted from the following student sample sentences. Rearrange the order of supportive statements from the least to the most important. If some of the ideas are of equal importance, indicate this by the choice of glue words.

CONTROLLING IDEA: For too long cigarette smokers have had their way and lit up their "cancer sticks" anywhere they wanted causing problems for non-smokers. Because of this, smoking cigarettes should be prohibited in public places where non-smokers gather and share the same air as smokers.

1. The elimination of smoking serves as a safety precaution by eliminating the chance of fires which destroy property and kill people.
2. When a person smokes, he leaves ashes and butts behind. These remnants slop everywhere causing clothing to get dirty from the mess.
3. The smoke from cigarettes blends into non-smokers' clothing causing a foul odor.
4. A non-smoker can develop cancer just as easily as a smoker by being in a smoke filled room inhaling the dangerous fumes.
5. The smoke from cigarettes causes unsanitary situations and makes it uncomfortable for the non-smoker who probably doesn't ask the smoker to stop. This is especially true for individuals suffering from lung and heart disease.
6. To solve this problem, the government should pass a law which would allow the non-smokers the same rights and privileges as smokers and give a heavy fine to anyone who violates this law.
7. When it comes right down to it, smokers not only hurt themselves, but they hurt innocent bystanders as well.

Ending

The ending should be part of the overall strategy of this paper. The ending may be a restatement of the controlling idea, or the writer may summarize all the supportive proofs. The writer may also choose to end the paper by the weight of the last argument. If so, a summary is not necessary as the impact of the final statement ends the paper. Finally, the writer may also wish to draw a conclusion or make a comment as the writer did in the sample compositions which follow.

EXERCISE 4: Before writing your first draft, study the sample compositions. The questions that follow the second composition can be used as a guide for class discussion.

Why Dogs Should Be Kept on a Leash

1. Ever since people have kept dogs as pets, others have been bothered by the unleashed animals. 2. Many problems are created by dogs that are not kept on leashes. 3. First of all, a great number of dogs are killed by running out into the street where unaware motorists accidentally hit them. 4. Every year hundreds of family pets are lost by wandering off too far. 5. Not only can harm come to the dogs themselves, but they can cause injury to people and damage to property as well. 6. Flower and vegetable gardens are often trampled by stray dogs. 7. They also make messes on parkways and lawns that attract flies and other insects as well as upsetting unsuspecting pedestrians who discover it all too late. 8. Such messes are nearly impossible to clean from the grass or one's shoes. 9. Additionally, loose dogs breed with other pets that may be kept chained outside for the night. 10. This results in unwanted puppies which sometimes end up in an animal shelter where they are likely to be put to sleep. 11. When female dogs must scrounge for food, they go through garbage cans and their pups can become diseased. 12. Other loose dogs are menacing when they chase children or postal employees. 13. If these dogs are rabid, the victims may need painful shots to combat the disease. 14. Both people and their animals are better off when their pets are kept on chains or leashes.

Take Us to Your Leader

1. Since the beginning of the space age and "sightings" of UFO's, the question has arisen as to whether or not there is life on planets. 2. Although many people doubt and scoff at the idea, life does exist on planets other than the earth. 3. In South America near Peru's Andes Mountains, there lie many huge and strange markings, not unlike those of an airfield, which, because of their size, can be seen only from the sky. 4. Supporters of UFO's and other strange phenomena argue that the

Peruvian Indians who carved these strange and ancient markings into the earth had not acquired the technology to be able to accomplish such a feat. 5. This supports the theory that possibly some extraterrestrial beings who visited the earth long ago may have influenced the Indians to build such structures to serve as airstrips. 7. Another strange case, described by Erik Von Daniken in his book *Chariots of the Gods*, tells of the findings of remains of an ancient storage battery believed to be many thousands of years old. 7. Quite obviously the men in that period did not possess the knowledge or ability to build such a gadget on their own, and believers of space phenomena attribute this to the possibility that these beings from other planets do exist, and at various times, visited earth. 8. Thirdly, sometimes strange noises appear in the headphones of scientists who man the huge radio-telescopes throughout the world. 9. Some of these sounds possess a regular pattern and signify the belief that out in the universe, somewhere, there may be some intelligent life, possibly more civilized than earth's, that tries to contact another civilization. 10. Lastly, one of the major arguments of this issue, and the most mathematically accurate, lies in the fact that out in the universe, there float millions of stars, planets, and galaxies. 11. The universe dwarfs the earth, a tiny bit of rock circling a minor star at the edge on an average galaxy, in contrast to the huge and endless universe. 12. To think that the population of this minor and obscure planet, three billion people, exists alone in that vast space is a very shallow thought. 13. So don't be surprised if some day little green men jump out of a flying saucer and ask you to take them to your leader.

1. What is the controlling idea?
2. What does the writer have to prove? What are the key words?
3. How many proofs did the writer use to support the CI?
4. Was each proof specific?
5. How did the writer organize the paper?
6. What glue words did the writer use to show shift of ideas?
7. Was the writer consistent with the verb tenses?
8. What type of ending did the writer use?

Think Sheet

For your paper to have the greatest impact upon the reader, it is essential you complete the think sheet in order. Complete the first two items. List all facts, reasons, examples, and statistics which oppose your stance. This is easiest done by either talking with someone who believes the opposite of you, or by doing some library research on your topic. If your topic is not believed by everyone, there should be some articles in pamphlets, magazines, or newspapers which will give you some specific ideas to argue against. Then, for every item against, counter with one or more of your ideas for your stance. Continue with your facts, reasons, examples, and statistics to complete your proofs.

Avoid general statements which lack exact proof. For example, a student wrote a composition about how the Federal Communications Commission should not prosecute people who use microwave dishes to intercept cable TV signals. The first proof stated: "First, people who live in rural areas need the dishes to receive any TV reception." The writer needed to expand with specific details to explain WHY and WHERE this interception takes place. Avoid emotional statements when no proof is available.

In the same paper, the writer also stated, "It isn't fair that some people can be denied TV just because they live outside the city." We all know it "isn't fair." That is why we are writing this paper with specific facts, reasons, examples, and statistics. After writing the tentative controlling idea, organize your ideas in the order which will create the most impact on the reader.

Name _____ Period _____

ORDER OF IMPORTANCE THINK SHEET

1. What is the subject? _____

2. What is your opinion of this subject? _____
   _____

3. Jot down specific facts, reasons, examples, and statistics that refute your stance. Be specific. Then for each item against your stance, list one or more arguments for your stance. Avoid general statements which lack exact proof or statements which are based on emotion rather than provable facts. Expand your arguments whith specific details by answering the journalistic questions.

AGAINST	FOR	GLUE WORDS
1.		
2.		
3.		
4.		
5.		
6.		
7.		

TENTATIVE CONTROLLING IDEA _____
_____

HINT: Before writing the first draft, organize the ideas for your argument in an order of importance sequence. List appropriate glue words next to each item. Expand when necessary using the journalistic questions.

SPECIAL HINT: If you cannot list more ideas for your stance than you can against, change your topic! You don't feel strongly enough about it.

STAGE TWO: WRITING THE FIRST DRAFT

With your completed think sheet in front of you, write your first draft. Don't forget to skip every other line and number sentences.

Your main goal in this section is to get your ideas from the think sheet to your paper. Don't be concerned with mechanical errors just yet. Here is a review of some things to consider as you begin to write:

1. Begin with the thought that your reader knows nothing about your issue. The background you supply will lay the groundwork for your arguments.

2. Your controlling idea should plainly state the issue and your stance on it.

3. Follow the organizational plan you feel will impact the reader the most.

4. With each of your reasons, stop and ask yourself if you can expand it with specific examples, facts, reasons, or statistics. Use the journalistic questions to expand.

5. Make sure you use order of importance glue words to indicate your order of importance and the shift from one point to the next.

6. Keep the verbs in the same tense.

7. Make your ending an important part of the paper.

HINT: To check to see if you stressed your main point in each sentence, underline the main idea in each sentence.

SPECIAL HINT: To make this paper even more personal, it might help to write it in first person.

NOW WRITE YOUR FIRST DRAFT! Reread it carefully and circle main verbs.

Sentence Opening Sheet

Here are the symbols to put above each column on the sentence opening sheet:

var, frag (glue)	order of importance	tense	RO, var
	glue words	VP, Taboo	# of words
first four words	special	verbs	per sentence

Now that your first draft is completed and the sentence opening sheet is filled out, check each column for the following:

Column One — First Four Words
1. Do all my sentences begin with the same word or same sentence structure? Can I rearrange any of them to make them more interesting?
2. If I used first person point of view, do too many of my sentences begin with "I?"
3. Do any of my sentences begin with glue words which might mean the sentence is a fragment?

Column Two — Special
1. Did I use order of importance glue words to indicate importance and the shift from one idea to the next?

Column Three — Verbs
1. Are all my verbs in the same tense?
2. Do my verbs agree in number with my subjects?
3. Did I overuse the same verbs? (VP)

Column Four — Number of Words Per Sentence
1. Do any of my short choppy sentences need combination for smooth word flow?
2. Is there variety in sentence lengths?
3. Are any of my longer sentences run-ons?

STAGE THREE: REWRITING

Before you exchange papers for a peer edit, criticize this sample first draft as a class exercise. Use your checklist sheet or the questions from Exercise 3 to help. Give this poor writer some specific help. For example, tell him/her sentence 3 is a fragment. You might even rewrite it as a complete sentence. (**HINT:** Is there personal involvement in this paragraph by the writer?) Refer to proofreading marks on page 158 to note mechanical errors.

All this Spending

1. Too much money goes into making a space mission successful while very little money goes into feeding the poor and hungry in this country. 2. The care of human beings should be a top priority in our society. 3. Not sending spaceships into outer space. 4. The majority of people who waste a considerable amount of money each year on material needs. 5. These people do not give money to the poor. 6. The people of this nation waste too much food. 7. The government should do something about this. 8. Although we gained knowledge from outer space findings. 9. We should rather use this money for the poor. 10. One major contributor which provides a firm helping hand comes from the Salvation Army. 11. Many institutions set on supporting the poor including religious institutions and missionaries. 12. Even with these helpers, many hungry mouths await to be fed!

SUPPLEMENTAL EXERCISE: Rewrite the following sentences using a variety of glue words, WH words, ING words, and ED words to introduce the lesser idea. Greatest impact should be placed in the main sentence. Underline the main idea.

EXAMPLE: The book was a favorite of teenagers. It was loved by adults, too.

REWRITTEN: The book, which is a favorite of teenagers, **was loved by adults as well.**

or

The book, loved by adults, **was a favorite of teenagers.**

1. Its appearance caused comment by auto magazines. The DeLorean was produced for only a few years.

2. Many people rush home to watch soap operas. There are people who still dislike them.
3. Students do not keep clean lockers. Bugs and mice thrive within them.
4. The aircraft can achieve speeds of up to 900 mph. It weighs less than half as much as other planes its size.
5. Students often feel most comfortable in jeans and Tee shirts. Comfortable students do better in school.
6. Women make good police officers. They solve numerous crimes.
7. Homework is necessary. Homework requires self discipline on sunny days.
8. Mary Lou Retton won a gold medal in gymnastics. She was only 16 years old.
9. Pets require great care. Pets reward owners with loyalty.
10. UFO's have been seen recently. Scientists check each sighting carefully.

Peer Evaluation Using a Checklist Sheet

Exchange papers with a proofreading partner. Read his or her paper two or three times so you understand the content before you answer the questions on the checklist sheet.

Writer's Name _____

Corrector's Name _____

ORDER OF IMPORTANCE CHECKLIST

1. Write out the controlling idea in the space provided.

2. What are the key words that indicate the writer's stance on the issue?

3. What type of background information does the writer include?

4. How many arguments does the writer use to support the controlling idea? Number them on the first draft.

5. Are these arguments specific? If not, expand by giving the writer some of your ideas. Note any statistics which need to be double checked.

6. How did the writer organize the paper? Most to least? Least to most?

7. Circle all the glue words which indicate when one idea ends and another begins.

8. Indicate if any sentences should be combined or rearranged. **(IMPACT)**.

9. Are all the verbs in the same tense?

10. What type of ending did the writer use? Was it a strong ending to a series of strong arguments? If not, give the writer some help.

11. Were you convinced? What would it take to convince you?

12. Mark all mechanical errors. Read the paper backwards to check for fragments.

UNIT TEN — COMPARISON/CONTRAST PAPER

One of the main ways we have of expressing our ideas about something or someone is to compare and/or contrast them with something or someone similar in nature. For this assignment, you will be asked to compare or contrast something or someone familiar to you.

STAGE ONE: PREWRITING

Student Learning Objectives:

1. The student will write a controlling idea that states the two items and whether they are compared or contrasted.
2. The student will organize the paper in either the flip-flop or the block method.
3. The student will use reasons, facts, examples, or statistics in parallel structures.
4. The student will use appropriate glue words for parallel structures.
5. The student will end the paper with the final point of the comparison/contrast or a statement to summarize or comment on the main thrust of the paper.

Helpful Drills

Before selecting the subject of your paper and jotting down specific ideas, practice some special drills which will teach you how to write equal ideas. There are times when a writer wants to make ideas of equal importance so the reader can understand what is being said. The only way the writer can achieve this is by writing the ideas in balanced (PARALLEL) structures. Study the following examples of balanced structures.

Balanced Structures (Parallelism)

A. Nouns: Ivan Bucks collects **pennies, nickles, dimes**, and **quarters.**
B. Verbs: Helga **walked** up to the edge of the board, **took** a deep breath, **lifted** her arms, **raised** up on her toes, and **sprang** into the air.
C. ING Words: **Showering, shampooing**, and **shining** shoes are musts for going on a date.

D. Prepositional Phrases: Oscar looked for his missing glasses **under the bed, behind the couch,, and in the closet.**
E. WH Clauses: The girl **who is confident, who is courageous,** and **who is prepared** will be successful.
F. Series of Sentences: **Miss Fittish slammed the door. She threw her books on the desk. She blew her nose.**

You have already studied glue words which connect greater ideas with lesser ideas. The following glue words (boys fan) connect equal ideas:

Equal Idea Glue Words

but, or, yet, so for, and, nor

neither	nor
either	or
whether	or
both	and
not only	but (also)

EXERCISE 1: Combine the following sentences by using glue words that connect equal ideas. Punctuate correctly.

EXAMPLE: The sun is shining. The air is calm.

REWRITTEN: The sun is shining, **and** the air is calm.

1. The curtains were pulled shut. The school was empty.
2. Alvin Ashby has always lived in the city. His parents bought a home in the suburbs.
3. Biggie Molar has a toothache. He will see the dentist, Dr. I. Yankum.
4. Pat Cahull received a new Mercedes. He passed all his subjects with A's.
5. Rod Ketchum worked in the city sewer system. He attended night school.
6. I may take a trip to Mt. Rushmore. I may stay home.
7. The boys were given five jugs each. They had cut Mr. Atom's science class.
8. I had a chance to buy a ten speed racer. I decided on buying an ATC instead.
9. Bike riding enables me to see the sights of the city. It allows me to lose weight.
10. The canoe was old and leaky. We won the race.
11. The girls had never played on the team before. They won the first game of the season.

12. He was bigger and stronger than I. I let him kick sand in my face.
13. Girls are weaker than boys. Boys are putty in their hands.
14. My name was called to give the speech. I walked slowly up the aisle.
15. I will go to the party. I won't play childish games.

EXERCISE 2: Combine the following sentences into one by first subtracting the repeated pronouns and then combining by using a series of verbs.

EXAMPLE: Melissa sat still. **She** watched the bird. **She** dreamed of her freedom.

REWRITTEN: Melissa sat still, watched the bird, and dreamed of her freedom.

1. Walter Waleye baited the hook. He cast the line into the lake. He caught a thirty pound perch.
2. Clarence Von Longhorn wore a full dress suit. He had a monocle in his left eye. He tripped over the curb. He broke his leg.
3. The passengers climbed into the bus. They handed the driver their tickets. They fought their way to the rear seats.
4. The class is noisy. They cause trouble in the cafeteria. They stampede through the exit doors.
5. Wilma Watchmoor turned off the lights. She held onto the banister. She slowly walked up the creaky stairs.

EXERCISE 3: Combine the following sentences into one by using ING words, prepositional phrases, or WH clauses. Try writing two different versions of each set of sentences. Review the comma rules on pages 14 and 15.

EXAMPLE: The pilot closed the door. She put on her headset. She began her first solo flight.

REWRITTEN: Closing the door and putting on her headset, the pilot began her first solo flight. (ING words)

or

The pilot, who closed the door and put on her headset, began her first solo flight. (WH clause)

1. The lost child sobbed. He cried out for his mother. He was taken to the lost and found department.
2. The high winds blew dust over the washed clothes. They picked up bits of paper. They damaged the property.

3. Students come to Northbrook Jr. High in several ways. Some ride bikes. Some walk. Some take the bus. Some hitchhike.
4. Ross McNix iced the glasses. He skewered the olives. He poured the ginger ale.
5. Cassie checked the oil. She filled the gas tank. She wiped the windshields. She put air into the deflated tire.

EXERCISE 4: On a separate sheet of paper, expand each sentence with an equal idea.

EXAMPLE: He had a dollar in his pocket and _____.

REWRITTEN: He had **a dollar in his pocket** and **penny in his hand**.

1. **Not only** did he clean out the bathroom but also _____.
2. **Either** by washing dishes **or** _____, Cindy will raise ten dollars to buy a new blouse.
3. He failed salesmanship **and** _____.
4. The long haired girl **danced,** _____, **and** _____.
5. George Cheddar wanted to know **who to see,** _____, **and** _____.
6. **Smashed by the wind,** _____ **and,** _____, the garden was totally destroyed.
7. _____ **and to be honest** are the key ingredients of of good class officer.
8. A bee **buzzing in the garden,** _____ **and,** _____ bit Roberta on the nose.
9. **Neither Julie nor** _____ admitted to taking the cookies.
10. _____, _____, **and mowing lawns** are ways of earning summer spending money.

SPECIAL HINT: If you have any problems writing run-on sentences, review the rules on page 30.

Subject

The purpose of this paper is to compare or contrast two items which have some common element. Nobody would compare a row boat with a horse fly, but they would compare a row boat with a sail boat. You must decide whether you will write about similarities or differences of your two items.

Do not try to do both as it would make the paper more complicated than necessary. This paper will be most successful if a subject of limited nature about which you have personal knowledge is chosen. It is also important that you have knowledge of both of the subjects you want to compare or contrast. Some research may be necessary for accuracy of facts or statistics used. However, save the total research project for another time.

Another important limitation on your choice of subjects is interest. You need genuine interest on both sides of the topic for your paper to be successful. A student could write a paragraph about similarities of the flight controls in a 747 and a 767 — but not from personal experience, and probably not from interest. That student will be more successful in choosing a topic closer to his/her own knowledge and interest.

Suggested Topics

The following topics are far too general to be covered adequately in a short paper such as this one. Use them as general ideas which can point you in the direction of a more specific, limited topic.

1. Seasons of the year — winter sports versus summer sports in a favorite vacation spot.
2. Two sports of a similar nature, i.e., school basketball versus playground basketball.
3. Advantages of apartment living versus "house" living.
4. Brother and sister; two sisters; two brothers; two cousins.
5. Two products — which is better? toothpaste, pizza, cookies, floor cleaners, hamburgers.
6. Activities of junior high school and senior high school.
7. Two types of cars, boats, bicycles, or skateboards, etc.
8. Two close friends.
9. Two areas of the country — the coast versus Midwest; North versus South; East versus West.
10. Two movies, books, TV programs of a similar nature.
11. Two celebrities — rock stars, TV stars, radio personalities, movie stars, etc.
12. Why _____ fast food restaurant is better than _____. Name them.
13. Why hamburgers (or any food) is better cooked at home on the barbeque than on _____ fast food grill. Or the opposite argument.
14. Advantages of one computer over another computer.
15. Two vacation spots.

As a group activity, narrow down some of the topics listed above making them more specific and personal. For example, a general subject such as the differences in yesteryear and the present might be limited just to environment.

Controlling Idea

The controlling idea should mention the two items being compared or contrasted. The key words should state whether you are finding similarities or differences. You may choose to supply some background to move the reader gently and naturally to your controlling idea.

Sample Controlling Idea: Movies, books, and TV programs always illustrate how simple life was in the good old days. **If we examined the natural living environment of yesteryear and today, we would find it cleaner and healthier to return to the days of the past.**

Organizing the Paper

After you have selected and narrowed your subject, jot down all of your ideas using a "T" bar. The following is a sample "T" bar for the controlling idea just discussed.

SUBJECT: NATURAL LIVING ENVIRONMENT YESTERYEAR AND THE PRESENT

YESTERYEAR	PRESENT
1. clean, fresh air	1. smog in the air
2. clean waterways	2. oil slicks in lakes and rivers
3. clean city streets	3. debris and garbage everywhere
4. friendly people	4. unfriendly people caring only for their own kind
5. wide, open spaces	5. congested, crowded cities
6. quiet sounds of nature	6. sounds of cities, machinery, people

Once you jot down an idea for one aspect of the subject being compared or contrasted, you must jot down a corresponding idea for the second item. This will help you in organizing the paper. Try to list at least four or five itmes on each side of the "T". After completely exhausting your list of ideas, subtract the unnecessary items which do not fit with the subject. Which items in the previous example should be elimitated? Use only the ideas you are totally familiar with. If you are not sure of some facts or statistics, be sure to look them up for accuracy.

One way of organizing the paper is to write all of the information on the first subject found on one side of the "T." This is followed by writing all the information on the second subject, or the other side of the "T." This is called the **block method**. This organizational pattern is used if you want the reader to see the total picture of each item at one time. It is the easiest for the writer.

More interesting for the reader, the **flip-flop method**, examines both sides of an item before moving to the next item. Before writing your first draft, decide upon which organizational pattern you want to use. This will depend upon what you are trying to achieve with your paper.

You should also plan on how the points in your paper will be organized. Have some strategy in mind. Don't just write.

Gluing Ideas Together

In writing a comparison/contrast paper, be aware of the various methods of linking ideas. One method is by using glue words that show similarities or point out differences.

Glue Words to Show Similarities: similarly, likewise, in the same manner, equally, in a similar fashion.

EXAMPLE: "Magnum P.I." has a great deal of action. **Similarly**, much of the appeal of "Remington Steele" is the action involving the two stars.

Glue Words to Point Out Differences: yet, still, but, although, however, rather, on the contrary, whereas, nevertheless, on the other hand, despite, instead of.

EXAMPLE: In junior high school, students must always carry a hall pass to walk in the hall at times other than passing times. **However**, in senior high school students are allowed the freedom of walking in the hall without a pass.

Another way of gluing ideas is to repeat similar sentence patterns (**balanced structures**). This not only links ideas but also helps create impact through repetition of key words. Review your answers to EXERCISE 4 and note the use of these similar patterns in the model in EXERCISE 5.

Ending

Your paper should have an effective ending that is planned carefully just as you planned the introduction and body of your paper. For this composition, you may end with the final point of your comparison/contrast, or you may try to end with a statement that summarizes or makes a comment on the main thrust of your paper.

EXERCISE 5: Before writing your first draft, study the sample composition. Be able to answer the following questions.

1. What is the controlling idea?
2. How did the writer lead into the controlling idea?
3. What are the two items being compared/contrasted?
4. How many points did the writer include in his paper?
5. Was each point specific?
6. How did the writer glue together ideas? Did he use glue words? Did he repeat key ideas?
7. Was the writer consistent with his tenses?
8. What type of ending did the writer use?

This Dangerous World

1. Teenagers arrested for possession of marijuana! 2. Oil spilled into the Gulf of Mexico. 3. State Police hunt for escaped convicts! 4. Unemployment rate up! 5. Race riots break out in New York! 6. These headlines can be read on the front page of almost every daily newspaper. 7. Evil and crime have increased greatly, and this can be proven by comparing yesteryear to the present. 8. A century ago people could stroll around without any fear of being attacked or molested, but today an individual must take certain precautions before going out onto crime infested streets. 9. A century ago the land, air, and water had very little pollution

in them, but today unsightly garbage covers the streets, thick smog fills the sky from the exhaust of cars, and black oil coats the waterways. 10. A century ago men and women could be hired by farmers or businessmen for needed extra pay, but today men and women just sit on park benches, lie in gutters, and sit on chairs in employment offices waiting for opportunity to knock. 11. A century ago people followed the saying of "Love Thy Neighbor," but today people only "obey" the law if the neighbor has the same skin color, the same intelligence, and the same social and economic status. 12. As time marches on, mankind keeps drifting back to the primitive ages and is being trampled in the process. 13. It's a shame we never learn.

Think Sheet

By filling out both sides of the "T" bar, you ensure yourself complete coverage of each item listed. You want to be as specific as possible on the think sheet. By expanding the general idea covered, the reader can more readily follow your thinking. Study this example:

Evergreen gym facilities	Poynter gym facilities
1. good lockers	bad lockers

NO!!

1. spacious, freshly painted lockers with air vents	cramped, stinky, paint peeling lockers; broken doors + no security

BETTER

Name _____ Period _____

COMPARISON/CONTRAST THINK SHEET

1. What are the two items being compared or contrasted?

   A. _____ B. _____

2. What is their common element? _____
3. Jot down specific ideas for each item being compared or contrasted.

   A. _____   B. _____   Glue Words

   1. _____   _____   _____
   2. _____   _____   _____
   3. _____   _____   _____
   4. _____   _____   _____
   5. _____   _____   _____
   6. _____   _____   _____
   7. _____   _____   _____
   8. _____   _____   _____
   9. _____   _____   _____
   10. _____   _____   _____
   11. _____   _____   _____

Tentative controlling idea _____
_____
_____

SPECIAL HINT: Before writing your first draft, fill out a second think sheet organizing your ideas in the actual sequence in which they will appear on the first draft. Fill in the glue words you will use to shift from one idea to the next.

STAGE TWO: WRITING THE FIRST DRAFT

With your completed, ordered think sheet in front of you, write the first draft. Don't forget to skip every other line and number sentences. Here is a review of some things to consider.

1. Begin with either background information or a controlling idea which clearly states the two items to be compared or contrasted and whether they are similar or different.
2. Follow the organizational plan you feel will impact the reader as outlined on your think sheet.
3. With each item discussed, ask yourself how it could be expanded with specific examples, facts, reasons, or statistics. Use the journalistic questions to help you expand.
4. Make sure you use glue words which point out similarities or differences.
5. Keep verbs in the same tense.
6. Make your ending an important part of the paper.

NOW WRITE YOUR FIRST DRAFT! Reread it carefully and circle the main verbs.

Sentence Opening Sheet

Here are the symbols to put above each column on the Sentence Opening Sheet.

Var, Frag	glue	tense VP, Taboo	RO, Var
First Four Words	Special	Verbs	# of Words Sentence

After completing the Sentence Opening Sheet, check it for the following:

Column One   **First Four Words**
1. Do all my sentences begin with the same word or the same sentence structure?

2. Can I rearrange any of them to make them more interesting or to achieve more variety?

Column Two   **Special**
1. Did I use boys fan words to glue similar ideas together?
2. Did I use glue words to point out similarities or differences?

Column Three   **Verbs**
1. Are all my verbs in the same tense?
2. Do all my verbs agree in number with my subjects?
3. Did I overuse the same verbs? (VP)

Column Four   **Number of Words Per Sentence**
1. Is there variety in my sentence lengths?
2. Are any of my longer sentences run-ons?
3. Are any of my sentences overly long or awkwardly constructed?

STAGE THREE: REWRITING

Before you exchange papers for a peer edit, criticize this sample first draft as a class exercise. Use the questions from Exercise 5 as a guide. This is the most difficult paper to organize because you have two items to write about instead of one. Also, you have a choice of two very different organizational patterns; therefore, you have more to consider as you criticize the model which follows. Make your criticism specific to help the reader. For example, in sentence 1, the writer uses "among" when talking about two items. "Between" is the proper usage. Refer to proofreading marks on page 158 to note mechanical errors.

Two Schools

1. Eight grade grammar school at Wingfoot and Freshman year at Parket High can be contrasted to find out many differences among them. 2. Eight graders are the oldest in the school and looked up to. 3. While freshmen, on the other hand, are the youngest and are always put down. 4. Eight graders receive very little homework while freshmen got homework every night. 5. Freshman year you get plenty of discipline. 6. While in eighth grade, you're mostly on your own. 7. If you flunk a subject in grammar school, you don't have to go to summer school, if you flunked a subject in high school, you have to make it up in summer school or else. 8. In grammar school you had to get permission to go to

the bathroom while in high shcool they don't let you go. 9. Freshman year's tough, but eight grade's hard too so what you have to do is just work your hardest in both spots.

SUPPLEMENTAL EXERCISE: Correct the errors found in the following sentences. First, find the errors, and then use the skills of combination, rearrangement, subtraction, and expansion to create smooth word flow and impact on the reader. Be particularly mindful of run-ons, fragments, and faulty parallelism. (This is when words or phrases on either side of the boys fan word are unlike in structure.)

EXAMPLE: Sammy can be considered responsible, he remembers to do things and does them, yet Henry can be considered irresponsible, he remembers and does what he wants.

REWRITTEN: Sammy can be considered responsible, **for** he remembers to do things and does them well. **On the other hand**, Henry can be considered irresponsible, **for** he remembers only what he wants.

EXAMPLE: Riding a bike and **to swim** are excellent exercises.
(Faulty parallelism)

REWRITTEN: Riding a bike and **swimming** are excellent exercises.

or

To ride a bike and **to swim** are excellent exercises.

1. As a junior, Kory played on the basketball team and averaging thirteen points per game.
2. The leopard's extremely good eyesight enables him to spot his prey from afar. While the shark's eyesight which allows him to spot his prey in blue water.
3. Kim's job is to clean up the front room and dusting all the furniture.
4. Diana has two choices. She can keep on paying for repairs on the stove, she can buy a new one at Sears.
5. A slight drizzle fell during the entire tennis match, consequently there were many puddles causing the girls to slip and falling.
6. The sophomore could take French this year or waiting until the second semester began.
7. The boy in the corner was not only quiet but also looked serious.

8. **Gone With the Wind** is charming, exciting, and one that appeals to both young and older people.
9. President Wilson worked for patience, for prosperity, and that there shall be no more wars.
10. T.V. tennis has only one line, this line runs across the width of of the middle of the screen.
11. Attending The Citadel is said to teach cadets to be alert, obedience, and how to have good leadership.
12. At **Sears** you will find some items that are inexpensive and others which cost a lot.
13. Jesse was told to collect the books and that he should erase the board.
14. The Miami Dolphins have a quarterback who is crafty, intelligent and shows a great deal of speed.
15. The girls' athletic association sponsored a concert, it was a huge success, it made plenty of money.

Peer Evaluation Using A Checklist Sheet

Exchange first drafts with your proofreading partner. Read his or her paper two or three times so you understand the content before you begin marking or answering questions on the checklist sheet.

Writer's name _____

Corrector's name _____

COMPARISON/CONTRAST CHECKLIST

1. Write out the controlling idea in the space provided.

2. Does the writer give any background information? If so, what type?

3. What are the two items being compared or contrasted?

4. What is their common element?

5. How many points did the writer include about each item? Number them on the first draft.

6. Was the writer specific with each point? If no, indicate this on the first draft.

7. How did the writer organize the paper? Flip-flop? Block?

8. How did the writer glue ideas together? Circle glue words and underline repeated key words.

9. Indicate if any sentences should be combined or rearranged for **IMPACT.**

10. What type of ending did the writer use? Does it need to be strengthened?

11. Are all the verbs in the same tense? Are there any taboo words? Mark any errors on the first draft.

12. Mark any mechanical errors. Do a super job in correcting your partner's paper!!!

UNIT ELEVEN MOOD PAPER

What is a mood? We all experience a variety of moods daily because of the lives we lead. They may be triggered by an event we participated in. A championship game, a graduation rehearsal, a family reunion, or a tragedy of a close friend can be best remembered by the mood you felt at the time. Mood may result from an author's skillful creation in a particular piece of literature or film. In this paper, you will be asked to recreate a vivid mood you experienced during some event in your life.

STAGE ONE: PREWRITING

Student Learning Objectives

1. The student will write a controlling idea that names the day and cites the specific mood to be recreated.
2. The student will support specific ideas with mood words.
3. The student will use glue words to indicate a shift from one idea to the next.
4. The student will use a chronological, enumeration, or general to specific organization.
5. The student will end the paper with a sense of finality created either by ending with the last item or making a comment on the mood described.

Helpful Drills

Instead of working only on sentence combining skills, this time we will begin with work on some thinking exercises designed first to recreate a mood common to the class. Second, you will practice a method by which you can recall a specific experience and its mood to be used for this paper.

EXERCISE 1: Try this as a class exercise.

1. Think of a mystery or horror movie, book, short story, or poem. (HINT: Just about any poem or short story by Edgar Allen Poe can be used as a common piece of literature.
2. Identify a specific scene.
3. What was the dominant mood?
4. What was the physical setting?
   a. What could you see?

b. What could you not see?
   c. What could you hear?
   d. What could you smell?
   e. What could you touch?
5. What event was taking place?
6. Who and/or what was involved?
7. When did it take place — time of year, day?
8. How did the time of the event affect the character and the mood?
9. How did you (or the character) feel? How do you know?
10. Why did you (or the character) feel this way? How do you know?
11. What are some vivid adjectives which describe the mood? (HINT: exciting, enthusiastic, joyous, awesome, solemn, serious, sorrowful, disgusting, angry, anxiety, fearsome, panicked, etc.)

Subject

The subject of this paper is to describe the mood you and your classmates experienced on either the first day of a new school year or on the last day before summer vacation. The emphasis should be on the mood felt by you and other students, not on the events of that particular day.

EXERCISE 2: Ask yourself the questions from Exercise 1 for the day you have chosen to describe. These should provide a good memory from which to complete your think sheet.

Controlling Idea

Your controlling idea should include both the time of year and the dominant mood or moods felt by students. Since we all differ, it is quite possible for various moods to be experienced by different students at these two times in the school year. For ease, choose only two moods to describe. In the sample which follows, the subject and key words are highlighted.

SAMPLE CONTROLLING IDEA: Even the most casual of shoppers could not help but be infected by the **frolicsome and jovial** atmosphere of **Santa's workshop.**

Organizing the Paper

As you begin to jot down strong feelings to show the moods of your specific time on your think sheet, include ideas about WHY these moods appear, HOW and in WHOM they show themselves, and WHAT actions reveal the students' feelings. Be specific and include activities that indicate these feelings. For example, an anxious student can be described as loud and noisy and shouting out answers, or constantly checking the clock on the wall, or fidgeting with books and moving the desk back and forth. A usually happy-go-lucky student might appear especially quiet and serious studying in the library or carefully reading a final homework assignment in the school's cafeteria.

Your paper should be organized by describing the prevailing moods and showing student activities that indicate these moods rather than giving personal testimony. After your think sheet is completed, organize the paper in the sequence that accomplishes your goal.

Gluing Together Ideas

In this paper you must be extremely careful to show the shift from one idea to the next by properly using glue words and by having your ideas organized in a logical order. In some instances your ideas might flow together by the natural listing of your student activities to indicate mood. Here is list of glue words that could prove helpful:

GLUE WORDS: Also, another, besides, furthermore, moreover, in addition, again.

TABOO WORDS (TEACHER OPTION): is, are, was, were, have, has, had, got, get, I, we, us, our, my, mine, you, your.

Ending

The ending of this paper should leave the reader with the prevailing mood or moods of the day you described. The reader should sense the paper is over. You might end on the last item in your listing, or you might comment on the meaning of the day to the students.

EXERCISE 3: Study the student model of a mood paper before filling out your think sheet. Answer the following questions:

1. What is/are the dominant mood(s) of the paper?
2. What event is described?

3. Who are the main participants in this event?
4. What activities of the participants indicate the dominant mood?
5. How did each participant feel?
6. What words indicate their feelings?
7. How was the paper organized?
8. How did the writer indicate a shift of ideas?
9. Why did the writer end the paper just before the beginning of the assembly?

The Election

1. A visitor walking through the halls of Kennedy Junior High School can feel the anticipation and excitement which fill the air as the school prepares for i*t*s student council election. 2. A group of seventh graders busily hang campaign posters, blue and gold streamers, balloons, and pictures of candidates. 3. Student election judges carefully prepare ballots, ballot boxes, and voting booths. 4. Student campaign managers excitedly boast of the accomplishments of their candidates over the school's public address system. 5. Moderators diligently explain the voting procedure to their excited homerooms. 6. PTA volunteers don their poll-watchers' armbands as the principal calls the homerooms to assemble in the auditorium. 7. The nervous candidates grasping their final speeches with sweaty palms ascend the stage steps and await the start of the asembly. 8. Within a few moments the assembly will begin and all the hard work will be over.

Think Sheet

Review your answers to Exercise 2 before beginning the think sheet. Limit yourself to the two dominant moods of the day. Use specific adjectives, adverbs, and verbs to convey the moods. Expand with great detail the specific activities which show the mood. After the think sheet is complete, organize your ideas in an order so as to best describe the mood or moods of the day. Finally, supply glue words to indicate the shift from one action to the next.

Name _____ Period _____

MOOD THINK SHEET

1. Are you describing the first day of a new school year or the last day before summer vacation? _____

2. What is/are the dominant mood(s) of this day? Limit your paper to two moods. _____

3. Jot down specific activities to support your dominant moods. If you need additional ideas, refer back to Exercise 2.

Specific activities to show mood	Mood words to convey feelings	Glue Words
a.		
b.		
c.		
d.		
e.		
f.		
g.		
h.		
i.		

Tentative Controlling Idea _____

SPECIAL HINT: Organize your ideas. This will depend upon your dominant mood(s) and what student activities you have jotted down to show these moods.

STAGE TWO: WRITING THE FIRST DRAFT

Keep your think sheet in front of you as you write your first draft. Make sure the activities indicate the dominant moods by carefully including key words to show how people feel. Make sure to skip lines and number your sentences.

Here are some things to remember:

1. Begin with the controlling idea that names your subject and key words.
2. Follow your organizational pattern as you determined on your think sheet.
3. Make sure the activities indicate the dominant mood by carefully including key words to show how people feel.
4. Expand with the journalistic questions "who," "what," "when," "where," "why," and "how" so the reader senses the feelings of the students.
5. Link your ideas using glue words.
6. Keep your verbs in the same tense.
7. End with the final item on your list or a comment on the effect of the mood on the students.

NOW WRITE YOUR FIRST DRAFT! Reread it carefully and circle each main verb.

Sentence Opening Sheet

Here are the symbols to put above each column on the sentence opening sheet:

var, frag	mood/ glue words	tense, VP Taboo	RO, var
First four words	special	verbs	# of words per sentence

Now that your first draft is completed and the sentence opening sheet is filled out, check each column for the following:

Column One   **First Four Words**
   1. Do all my sentences begin with the same word or sentence structure? Can I rearrange any of them to make them more interesting?
   2. Do any of my sentences begin with glue words or ING words making them perhaps fragments?

Column Two   **Special**
   1. Did I use glue words to indicate a shift from one idea to the next?
   2. Did I include mood words to indicate a dominant mood(s)?

Column Three   **Verbs**
   1. Are all my verbs in the same tense?
   2. Do I repeat the same verbs over and over again?
   3. Did I use any taboo words?

Column Four   **Number of Words Per Sentence**
   1. Do any of my short, choppy sentences need to be combined to make them more interesting?
   2. Are any of my overly long sentences run-ons?
   3. Do I have a variety of senntence lengths?

STAGE THREE: REWRITING

Feelings

1. A week before graduation many mixed emotions fill the air and ideas cloud many minds. 2. The minds of kids, who in a week, will graduate after eight years of hard work. 3. Every person who graduates has different feelings toward graduation. 4. Classmates are saddened by the thought of hardly seeing their friends after they graduate. 5. Other kids wonder if they will graduate. 6. Also they are wondering how high school will be, wondering if they will be accepted, and wondering what the new teachers will be like. 7. The teachers find so much has to be done in so little time, they must prepare tests and they must fill out report cards. 8. Yet other kids are impatient for that one special day to come when they will leave the school they knew so well. 9. Still other kids leave not caring or worring about teachers and classmates. 10. But mostly this is a time of happiness. 11. Happy because it is finally over.

SUPPLEMENTAL EXERCISE: These sentences contain run-on and fragment errors which can be corrected by using the skills of combination, rearrangement, subtraction, and expansion. Eliminate the words indicated as taboo by your teacher.

EXAMPLE: Not checking with the weather station. Pilots get into difficulties when storms arise. (The fragment is eliminated by combining and expanding.)

REWRITTEN: By not checking with the weather station, pilots get into difficulties when storms arise. (The fragment is eliminated by combining and expanding.)

1. As the school doors close, the swimming pools are filled with fresh blue water. Welcoming school kids who wait for a hot June summer.
2. Nobody who likes the month of September. Especially junior high students.
3. Boys run down the halls, screaming and shouting they slam their locker doors for a last time.
4. While skateboards fill the streets and kids follow the ice cream truck.
5. Because September rarely brings a smile to faces when it comes.
6. The most commotion of the year, school being dismissed.
7. All the kids wait for June. Which is a happy and fun month because summer vacation begins.
8. They feel glad too because they can also rest students feel nice on the last day.
9. The students wait for the bell to end school they run crazily out of the building they dive into the pool which hasn't been filled yet.
10. In the beginning of the year there is a feeling of fear. Because school started at the beginning of the year in September.

Peer Evaluation Using a Checklist Sheet

Exchange papers with a proofreading partner. Read his or her paper two or three times so you understand the content before you answer the questions on the checklist sheet.

Writer's Name _____

Corrector's Name _____

MOOD PAPER CHECKLIST

1. Write out the controlling idea in the space provided. Mark the key words.

2. What time of year is the writer describing?

3. What are the moods indicated in the controlling idea?

4. How many activities does the writer include to support the key words? Number them on the first draft.

5. Are these activities specific? Does the writer include mood words – adjectives, adverbs, and verbs – to color the activities described?

6. How was the paper organized? Did the writer use a chronological sequence or enumerate (list) the ideas?

7. Are there any gaps? Do the ideas shift too rapidly? If so, mark the spots on the first draft.

8. Circle all glue words which indicate a shift of ideas on the first draft.

9. Check the writer's verb choices and verb tense consistency.

10. Did the writer use any taboo words? Mark them on the first draft.

11. Indicate if any sentences should be combined or rearranged for **IMPACT**.

12. What type of ending did the writer use? Is it the last item on the list or a comment on the meaning of the day?

13. Mark all mechanical errors. Check for fragments and run-ons.

English Composition Correction Symbols

ABR	abbreviation needed or abused
S-V AGR	subject and verb agreement needed; a singular subject with a plural verb or vice versa
CAP	capitalization
DM	dangling modifier
FRAG	fragment
GAP	an idea has been skipped; something is missing
IMPACT	combine or rearrange to stress an idea
LINK	glue word needed; weak bridging of ideas
LOG	illogical; ideas do not follow
PARA	new paragraph needed; indent
//	awkard structure; ideas do not balance; faulty parallelism
POSS	possession
PUNC	punctuation
REF	reference unclear; pronoun and antecedent confused
REP	useless repetition; subtract unnecessary idea
RO	run-on sentence; lack of proper punctuation
SPEC	vague ideas; be specific; expand
SP	spelling
VAR	variety needed in sentence openings or lengths
VP	verb power; create impact with verbs
VT	verb tense inconsistency; jumping from past to present, etc.
WC	poor word choice
WF	awkward word flow
YUK	SNOW JOB!!! GET A SHOVEL!!! DULLSVILLE!!! BUTTERSCOTCH!!!!